DISCOVERING THE PREHISTORIC WORLD

DISCOVERING
THE PREHISTORIC
WORLD

A guide to the
astonishing
forms of early
life on Earth

Marianne Taylor

SIRIUS

SIRIUS

This edition published in 2023 by Sirius Publishing, a division of
Arcturus Publishing Limited,
26/27 Bickels Yard, 151–153 Bermondsey Street,
London SE1 3HA

Copyright © Arcturus Holdings Limited

ISBN: 978-1-3988-3053-0
AD010549US

Printed in China

Contents

Introduction..6

Chapter 1: The Archean and Proterozoic Eons.....................8
    Overview of the eons..................................10
    Formation of Earth and the Solar System.................12
    Pre-life Earth..14
    The chemistry of life.................................16
    RNA World..18
    The first living organisms............................20
    Oxygenating the Earth.................................22
    The origin of eukaryotes..............................24
    Multicellularity.....................................26
    The advent of animals.................................28

Chapter 2: The Paleozoic Era....................................30
    Overview of the era..................................32
    Geographical flux....................................34
    The Cambrian explosion...............................36
    Mysteries of the Burgess Shale.......................38
    Trilobites and ammonites.............................40
    The first chordates..................................42
    The first marine plants..............................44
    Setting foot on land—breathing the air...............46
    Mosses, lichens and fungi............................48
    Soil formation and early land ecosystems.............50
    Bones and teeth—the first vertebrates................52
    Reaching for the skies—large land plants.............54
    The first forests....................................56
    Giant invertebrates of the Carboniferous.............58
    Emergence (literally) of land vertebrates............60
    Free from the water—the essential amniote sea.....62
    Paleozoic ice ages...................................64
    Pangaea..66
    The Permian mass extinction..........................68
    A handful of survivors—the founders of
      Mesozoic life......................................70

Chapter 3: The Mesozoic Era.....................................72
    Overview of the era..................................74
    A radiation of ray-finned fish.......................76
    Triassic triumphs—early archosaur groups.............78
    The slow return of continents........................80
    Reefs and reptiles of the sea........................82
    Tropical land vertebrates............................84
    The first true mammals...............................86
    Dispersal through the end of Pangaea.................88
    A not-so-mini mass extinction........................90
    Gymnosperms—a new way to be a plant..................92
    Dinosaurs—the sauropods..............................94
    Dinosaurs—early meat-eating bipeds...................96
    Dinosaurs—Stegosaurus & other ornithischians.....98

An explosion of mammal diversity....................100
Marine giants—plesiosaurs and more....................102
The first eutherian mammals..........................104
Jurassic dark—extinctions in the mid–Mesozoic.106
The rise of sharks and rays..........................108
Modern insect groups appear..........................110
Octopuses and other sea invertebrates.................112
The first flowering plants...........................114
The first feathers...................................116
The first true birds.................................118
Cretaceous dinosaur diversity—an overview.........120
Dinosaurs—T. rex and other giant carnivores.........122
Dinosaurs—Triceratops and other horn-bearers...124
Dinosaurs—an array of theropods......................126
Dinosaurs—the challenge of reconstruction..........128
Dinosaurs—behaviour..................................130
New insect groups emerge.............................132
Marine reptile diversity in the late Mesozoic..........134
    Pterosaurs.......................................136
Other land reptiles..................................138
Co—existence of marsupials and eutherian
    mammals..140
Birds of the late Cretaceous.........................142
The Cretaceous—Paleogene mass extinction.........144
What caused it?......................................146
Survivors and casualties.............................148

Chapter 4: The Cenzoic era..................................150
    Overview of the era.................................152
    Placental mammal radiation.........................154
    Sharks rule the oceans.............................156
    Forests flourish from pole to pole.................158
    The advent of "big birds"..........................160
    Snakes and lizards.................................162
    Crocodilians.......................................164
    Early primates.....................................166
    Grasses and grazers................................168
    A great many great whales..........................170
    Seals take to the water............................172
    Flowers and animals................................174
    The evolution of apes..............................176
    Mammalian megafauna................................178
    Continental drift, evolution in isolation..........180
    A cooling planet...................................182
    Stasis and change..................................184
    The first humans...................................186
    Modern genera......................................188

Glossary...190
Index..191
Picture credits..192

// Introduction

Humankind first began to create imagery as a means of communication some 7,500 years ago. The writing, back then, was literally on the wall. It began with cave art, and then was engraved into stone blocks. These first proto-languages used pictures as literal depictions of events, and this evolved into a system of simpler symbols that were representative of the sounds used in speech. Through writing, our ancestors were able to create a lasting record—a history. What exactly they chose to record in this way varied from the mundane to the significant, and all of this diversity adds to the richness of our understanding of how humans once lived, and what they lived through.

However, these 7,500 years capture only the most recent snapshot of our species' own history, as we know that anatomically modern humans have existed for at least 100,000 years. And even these earliest true humans have existed for an eyeblink of time in relation to the history of life on Earth, which stretches back another 3.7 billion years. Their history was never recorded by intention, but their existence is nevertheless revealed through the traces they have left behind—traces that have survived through all those millennia to be examined by curious human eyes today.

Above *Ammonites died out at the same time as the dinosaurs, but left behind beautiful and abundant fossils.*

Stories in stone

A piece of shale, carefully chipped away from its parent rock, reveals the beautiful whorled imprint of a long-dead marine animal. This creature, an ammonite, died and was buried in the settling particles of sediment that eventually formed this rock. Its soft tissues decomposed entirely, but its hard shell survived longer, and was mostly replaced over time with different minerals, producing a distinct and detailed impression. Fossils like this can be found in many parts of the world, although fossilization is itself a very rare process. Palaeontology, the study of fossils, has revealed the astounding diversity of the life that existed on our planet long before we came along, and has enabled us to build a timeline of when key lineages first appeared (and disappeared).

Palaeontology brings us as close as we can get to those long-lost life forms. The fossil of an animal reveals much more than overall structure—it can tell us about the animal's abundance and distribution, habitat, lifespan, growth pattern and may even shed some light on aspects of behavior. Through fossil discoveries, we can be reasonably sure, for example, that the small dinosaur *Microraptor* flew like a biplane and caught prey as varied as fish, birds and mammals, while *Oviraptor* incubated its eggs and provided extended care to its young, just as modern birds do. However, palaeontology is just one of many scientific disciplines that enable us to explore and understand prehistoric life on Earth.

The past captured

When we think of fossil hunters, we picture Victorians toiling with hammer, chisel and brush in dusty quarries, to eventually unearth some spectacular finds. In stark contrast, the work of geneticists primarily takes place in the lab and requires high-powered tech and computer analysis to provide a comprehensible interpretation. Genetic research on organisms that are alive today provides another window into the past. By comparing the genomes of two species, we can calculate how long ago their last common ancestor lived, and eventually build a detailed and time-stamped evolutionary tree for all life on Earth.

Studying the anatomy of extinct and living species also allows us to chart the course of evolution. For example, an inspection of skeletal anatomy combined with genetics reveals that that modern whales' closest living relatives are hoofed mammals such as cows, deer and (particularly) hippopotamuses, and through this insight we can infer more about when and how the whale lineage first took to the water. Biogeography—the distribution of living and fossil life on Earth—coupled with the study of plate tectonics,

Above Microraptor, *a Cretaceous dinosaur with four feathered wings.*

show how living things have spread around our planet, aided and abetted by the slow-motion remodeling of oceans and landmasses over deep time. Geologists know that inorganic rock itself is worn down and rebuilt through time and carries a memory of events such as continental plate collisions, volcanic eruptions, floods, and meteor strikes—all of which have had lasting effects on living things.

Stories of past and present

From their fossils, their hidden genetic past, and the traits they share with living relatives, we can recreate imagery of long-lost plants and animals from prehistory. Some of these are even more familiar now than many of those species that are still with us. *Tyrannosaurus rex*, woolly mammoth and mighty Megalodon are household names in many cultures, and the likes of trilobites and ammonites, pterosaurs and plesiosaurs, and *Archaeopteryx* and *Smilodon* are right behind them.

However, our interpretations of them have evolved as our knowledge has increased. No longer does *Tyrannosaurus* lumber along in an awkwardly upright posture with its tail dragging behind it, and no longer does the dodo wait, bloated, absurd, and helpless, to meet its inevitable end. Prehistory teaches us that all species evolved as successful, well-adapted citizens of their particular environments, but that environmental change exposes those adaptations to a constant barrage of challenges. Under the harsh husbandry of natural selection, the tree of life continues to grow, branch, and spread, but at the same time parts of it are always withering away. Through our understanding of astrophysics, we know now when life on our planet was born and when it will die, and in this knowledge, we can look back and forward from a position of great privilege. This book tells the prehistory of life on Earth as we know it, from uncertain and speculative beginnings through biochemistry, up until our own species first began to record a history of its own.

THE ARCHEAN AND PROTEROZOIC EONS

When it first formed, our world was violently hostile to life as we know it, with non-stop volcanic activity, intensely high temperatures, and a toxin-laden atmosphere. However, the first precursors to life appeared surprisingly quickly, and evolved into a diversity of single-celled organisms, all possessing efficient biochemical equipment to utilize what resources existed. As they spread and thrived, and began to form associations with one another, they formed Earth's first ecosystems. Their presence and metabolic processes gradually but completely changed the make-up of Earth's surface and atmosphere, forming what we now call the biosphere, and paving the way for more complex life to appear.

Microbial mats surrounding Grand Prismatic Spring in the Midway Geyser Basin of Yellowstone National Park, Wyoming, USA.

// Overview of the eras

The early history of the Earth, covered in this chapter, takes us from when the Earth was formed, some 4,540 million years ago, to the beginning of the Paleozoic Era, 538.8 million years ago (MYA). The first 500 million years of this vast tract of geological time is defined as the Hadean Eon, and it pre-dates the emergence of life on Earth. With the first appearance of living organisms, there then followed the Archean Eon, from 4,000 to 2,500 MYA, and the Proterozoic Eon, from 2,500 to 538.8 MYA. For most of this timespan, only single-celled organisms existed—initially these were simple prokaryotes, including bacteria, with the more complex (but still single-celled) early eukaryotes appearing some 2,700 million years ago. The first multicellular organisms appeared some 2,100 million years ago, well into the Proterozoic Era.

By most definitions, the Hadean Eon is not divided into eras. However, the Archean Eon is divided into four eras—Eoarchean, Paleoarchean, Mesoarchean and Neoarchean, each encompassing about 400 million years; and the Proterozoic Eon is divided into three eras—Paleoproterozoic (2,500 to 1,600 MYA), Mesoproterozoic (1,600 to 1,000 MYA) and Neoproterozoic (1,000 to 538.8 MYA).

The Hadean, Archean and Proterozoic Eons between them encompass more than 88 percent of the 4,540 million years that have elapsed since the formation of the Earth. The end of the Proterozoic Eon is traditionally marked by the first appearance of true animal life, although we know now that many early animals did first appear in the later part of the Proterozoic Era, primarily during the last 100 million years of the Neoproterozoic Era, in what is known as the Ediacaran Period. It is still true to say that the majority of familiar animal lineages, and certainly all vertebrate animals, emerged during the fourth and current geological eon—the Phanerozoic.

As vertebrate animals ourselves, we naturally feel a particular interest in the evolutionary history of our own lineage. It is hard for us to fathom that only single-celled life existed on Earth for so many millions of years. However, the earlier eons of our planet's history saw the emergence within simple organisms of a huge array of vital microscopic structures, biochemical processes, and ecologies that allowed more complex life to develop. These millennia also saw the fabric of our planet and its atmosphere go through enormous change. The life that existed through those times was at the mercy of these capricious conditions, but in the wake of disaster came opportunity, and the course of life's history was determined by how organisms adapted to the roller coaster of change on which they found themselves.

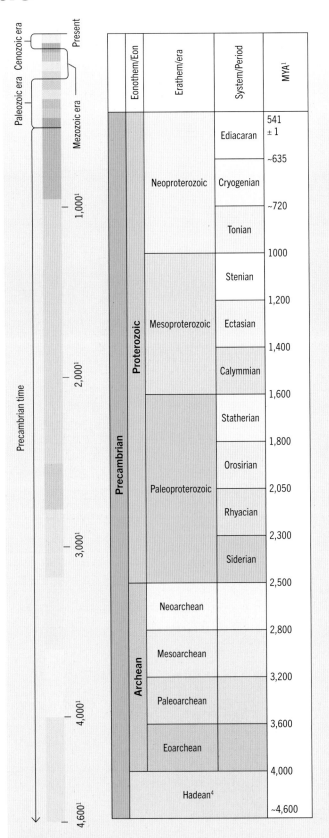

Eonothem/Eon	Erathem/era	System/Period	MYA[1]
Precambrian	Proterozoic	Neoproterozoic	Ediacaran	541 ± 1
			Cryogenian	~635
			Tonian	~720
		Mesoproterozoic	Stenian	1000
			Ectasian	1,200
			Calymmian	1,400
		Paleoproterozoic	Statherian	1,600
			Orosirian	1,800
			Rhyacian	2,050
			Siderian	2,300
	Archean	Neoarchean		2,500
		Mesoarchean		2,800
		Paleoarchean		3,200
		Eoarchean		3,600
				4,000
		Hadean[4]		~4,600

[1] Millions of years ago.
[2] Both the Mississippian and Pennsylvanian time units are formally designated as subperiods within the Carboniferous Period.
[3] Several Cambrian unit age boundaries are informal and are awaiting ratified definitions.
[4] The Hadean Eon is an informal interval of geologic time.

Geologic time scale

Note: In each table the MYA[1] values are printed at the stage boundaries; below, each value is shown with the stage at whose base it appears. The uppermost boundary value is given as a note above each table.

Table 1 — top boundary: 358.9 ± 0.4 MYA

Econothem/Eon	Erathem/Era	System/Period	Series/Epoch	Stage/Age	MYA[1]
Phanerozoic	Paleozoic	Devonian	Upper	Famennian	372.2 ± 1.6
				Frasnian	382.7 ± 1.6
			Middle	Givetian	387.7 ± 0.8
				Eifelian	393.2 ± 1.2
			Lower	Emsian	407.6 ± 2.6
				Pragian	410.8 ± 2.8
				Lochkovian	419.2 ± 3.2
		Silurian	Pridoli		423 ± 2.3
			Ludlow	Ludfordian	425.6 ± 0.9
				Gorstian	427.4 ± 0.5
			Wenlock	Homerian	430.5 ± 0.7
				Shienwoodian	433.4 ± 0.8
			Llandovery	Telychian	438.5 ± 1.1
				Aeronian	440.8 ± 1.2
				Rhuddanian	443.8 ± 1.5
		Ordovician	Upper	Hirnantian	445.2 ± 1.4
				Katian	453 ± 0.7
				Sandbian	458.4 ± 0.9
			Middle	Darriwilian	467.3 ± 1.1
				Dapingian	470 ± 1.4
			Lower	Floian	477.7 ± 1.4
				Tremadockan	485.4 ± 1.9
		Cambrian[3]	Furongian	Stage 10	~489.5
				Jianshanian	~494
				Paibian	~497
			Series 3	Guzhangian	~500.5
				Drumian	~504.4
				Stage 5	~509
			Series 2	Stage 4	~514
				Stage 3	~521
			Terreneuvian	Stage 2	~529
				Fortunian	541 ± 1.0

Table 2 — top boundary (Tithonian): −145 MYA

Econothem/Eon	Erathem/era	System/Period	Series/Epoch	Stage/Age	MYA[1]
Phanerozoic	Mesozoic	Jurassic	Upper	Tithonian	152.1 ± 0.9
				Kimmeridgian	157.3 ± 1
				Oxfordian	163.5 ± 1
			Middle	Callovian	166.1 ± 1.2
				Bathonian	168.3 ± 1.3
				Bajocian	170.3 ± 1.4
				Aalenian	174.1 ± 1
			Lower	Toarcian	182.7 ± 0.7
				Pliensbachian	190.8 ± 1
				Sinemurian	199.3 ± 0.3
				Hettangian	201.3 ± 0.3
		Triassic	Upper	Rhaetian	~208.5
				Norian	~227
				Carnian	~237
			Middle	Ladinian	~242
				Anisian	247.2
			Lower	Olenekian	251.2
				Induan	251.902 ± 0.024
	Paleozoic	Permian	Lopingian	Changhsingian	251.14 ± 0.7
				Wuchiapingian	259.1 ± 0.5
			Guadalupian	Capitanian	265.1 ± 0.4
				Wordian	268.8 ± 0.5
				Roadian	272.95 ± 0.11
			Cisuralian	Kungurian	283.5 ± 0.6
				Artinskian	290.1 ± 0.26
				Sakmarian	295 ± 0.18
				Asellian	298.9 ± 0.15
		Carboniferous	Pennsylvanian[2] Upper	Gzhelian	303.7 ± 0.1
				Kasimovian	307 ± 0.1
			Pennsylvanian[2] Middle	Moscovian	315.2 ± 0.2
			Pennsylvanian[2] Lower	Bashkirian	323.2 ± 0.4
			Mississippian[2] Upper	Serpukhovian	330.9 ± 0.2
			Mississippian[2] Middle	Visean	346.7 ± 0.4
			Mississippian[2] Lower	Tournaisian	358.9 ± 0.4

Table 3

Econothem/Eon	Erathem/Era	System/Period	Series/Epoch	Stage/Age	MYA[1]
Phanerozoic	Cenozoic	Quaternary	Anthropocene		1960 CE
			Holocene		0.0117
			Pleistocene	Upper	0.126
				Middle	0.781
				Calabrian	1.8
				Gelasian	2.58
		Neogene	Pliocene	Piancenzian	3.6
				Zanclean	5.333
			Miocene	Messinian	7.246
				Tortonian	11.63
				Serravallian	13.82
				Langhian	15.97
				Burdigalian	20.44
				Aquitanian	23.03
		Paleogene	Oligocene	Chattian	27.82
				Rupelian	33.9
			Eocene	Priabonian	37.8
				Bartonian	41.2
				Lutetian	47.8
				Ypresian	56
			Paleocene	Thanetian	59.2
				Selandian	61.6
				Danian	66
	Mesozoic	Cretaceous	Upper	Maastrichtian	72.1 ± 0.2
				Campanian	83.6 ± 0.2
				Santonian	86.3 ± 0.2
				Coniacian	89.8 ± 0.2
				Turonian	93.9
				Cenomanian	100.5
			Lower	Albian	~113
				Aptian	~125
				Barremian	~129.4
				Hauterivian	~132.9
				Valanginian	~139.8
				Berriasian	~145

// Formation of Earth and the Solar System

The planet Earth is one of eight true planets orbiting the star that we know as the Sun. The four innermost planets are small with a rocky surface, while the outermost four are large "gas giants" and "ice giants." The entire system was formed from part of a nebula—an interstellar cloud of gas and dust. We can observe other nebulae of various sizes in our galaxy today. Some are the debris left behind when stars have burned themselves out, but nebulae can also lead to the formation of new stars and planetary systems.

The nebula destined to become our Sun and its planets was shaped by gravity into a disc or solar nebula with most of the gas and dust collecting in the centre. This central, dense core of the disk became the Sun, with other objects forming around it through constant collision of particles that were then held together through gravity. In a similar way, once the early planets had accumulated enough mass to hold objects in their own orbits, moons began to form around most of them. The inner planets formed from compounds with high melting points, as the heat of the Sun was too much to allow water and other lightweight compounds to condense into a solid form. These inner planets are Mercury, Venus, Earth and Mars. Further out, the gas giants Jupiter and Saturn formed, and then the ice giants Uranus and Neptune. Their size is much greater than the rocky planets as the material that formed them was much more abundant in the solar nebula.

The Sun contains about 99.85 percent of all the mass of the Solar System, and the gas and ice giant planets hold 99 percent of the 0.15 percent remaining. The rocky material in the Solar System comprises the four rocky planets and numerous moons, but also a vast number of smaller objects, most of which are found in the asteroid belt (which lies between the orbits of Mars and Jupiter) and the Kuiper belt, which lies beyond the orbit of Neptune. Very early in Earth's history, it is theorized that a collision between Earth and another, smaller proto-planet known as Theia gave rise to the Earth's Moon. We think of moons as round because ours is, but only about 20 of the 200 or more moons in the Solar System have enough mass for their own gravity to pull them into a round shape—the rest have irregular shapes.

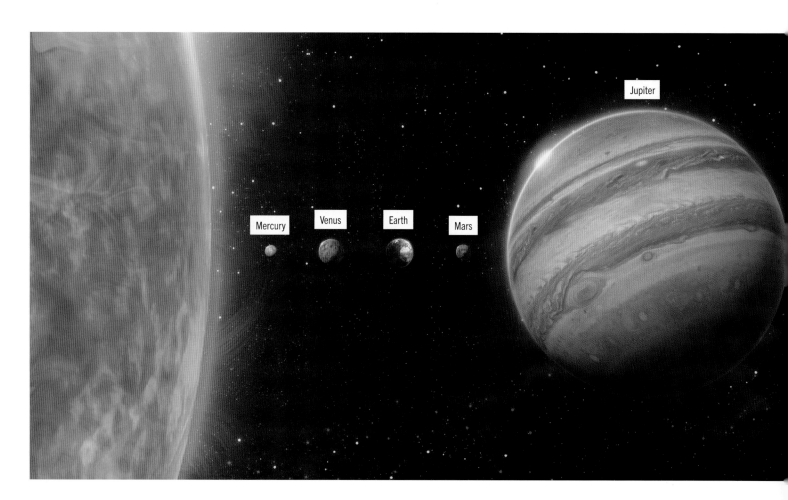

A WORLD-CHANGING ADDITION

Of the eight planets in our Solar System, only Mercury and Venus are moon-less. Mars has two, while the giant planets have many (Jupiter has 66!). Earth's moon is the fifth largest of the moons in our Solar System, but is by far the largest of them all relative to the size of its parent planet, at 1.2 percent the mass of Earth. Its gravitational interplay with the Earth stabilizes the Earth on its axis, and its pull causes our oceans to have tides. Illuminated by the Sun at night, it also provides a light source in dark skies. All three of these factors help make the Earth hospitable to a diversity of life.

Right *The Moon's reflected sunlight and gravitational pull has played a key role in shaping Earth's ecosystems.*

Below *The relative sizes of the eight true planets in our solar system.*

Saturn

Uranus

Neptune

// Pre-life Earth

The Hadean Era of Earth's geological history takes its name from Hades—the Greek god of the underworld, and also the name of his realm. In mythology, the realm of Hades was not specifically a place for evil souls to face punishment, and so was much more benign than the lake-of-fire Hell described in the Christian New Testament, but the Earth in the early Hadean Era was certainly a place where any mortal human would have suffered terribly (if briefly).

The Earth at that time was newly formed from condensed heavy, rocky compounds, and rock vapor formed much of its atmosphere for about 2,000 years. For many millennia after this had all condensed into solid material, the planet would have remained extremely hot, with a surface temperature of about 446°F (230°C), and a dense atmosphere composed mainly of carbon dioxide. This atmosphere would have exerted enough pressure on the planet to allow water to remain in a liquid state, so there would have been extensive, incredibly hot oceans. The Earth would also have been subject to intense bombardment from other smaller objects in the Solar System, and there would have been enormous inner turmoil too, as cooling, solidifying rock sank towards the core while molten rock surged to the surface.

The cooling process was rapid, though. The material of the Earth settled into the layered form that exists today, comprising a solid (due to enormous pressure) inner core of iron and nickel, a fast-churning liquid metal outer core, the thick mantle of slow-flowing molten silicon and metal above, and a relatively cool and stable thin rocky crust (with liquid water sitting on parts of it) enclosing all of this heat and energy. As the Earth's crust formed, so conditions on the surface became more stable. By 4.4 MYA, the surface temperature was below 212°F (100°C), and the distribution of oceans and land masses had become relatively settled. The planet's atmosphere also changed as carbon dioxide dissolved into ocean water.

CENTRAL HEATING

Hot and hellish though it was, the Hadean Earth was not a Sun-warmed place—its heat was the after-effect of its own very recent formation. However, that heat was to disappear rapidly, and the young Sun had far less heat (and indeed light) to impart. It was the Earth's atmosphere that prevented a rapid transition from hot-tub to ice-ball. Today, we know carbon dioxide as a "greenhouse gas"—trapping the Sun's heat in our atmosphere and warming our planet much more rapidly and dangerously than at any other time in our species' history. However, a carbon dioxide-rich atmosphere in the Earth's early history may have been a vital piece of the planetary puzzle that created life-friendly conditions. Within this prehistoric greenhouse, the atmosphere did what the Sun could not yet do, and kept the planet warm enough for surface water to remain liquid rather than become solid.

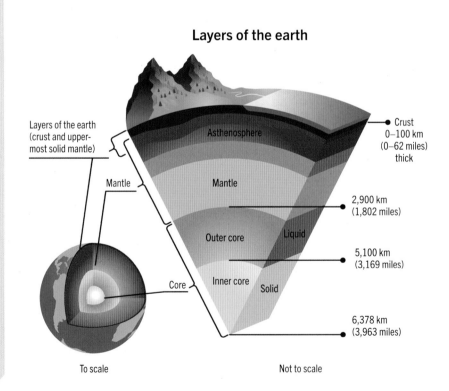

Layers of the earth

Layers of the earth (crust and uppermost solid mantle)

Mantle

Core

Asthenosphere

Mantle

Outer core   Liquid

Inner core   Solid

Crust 0–100 km (0–62 miles) thick

2,900 km (1,802 miles)

5,100 km (3,169 miles)

6,378 km (3,963 miles)

To scale   Not to scale

Above *The Earth's layers, as they are today. The mantle is rocky in nature while the core is mostly composed of iron.*

Opposite *Thankfully, the collision between Earth and Theia (resulting in the formation of the Moon) occurred before Earth was home to living things.*

// The chemistry of life

Our bodies contain about 36 different chemical elements, all originally formed through nuclear fusion reactions within our Sun. By definition, a chemical element cannot be broken down into a simpler substance, but the atoms of any given element can bond with other atoms (of the same element or a different one), to form compounds. Compounds have very different properties to the elements that form them—for example, in their pure states the element sodium is a soft metal and the element chlorine is a volatile green gas, but the compound they form together (sodium chloride) is a white crystalline solid that tastes good on fries.

Countless different compounds are found in the human body, and the vast majority of them are made of just four elements—carbon, oxygen, hydrogen and (to a lesser extent) nitrogen. Molecules that contain carbon are known as "organic" because of their association with living things, and they include sugars, starches, fatty acids and proteins, which all have vital roles in living systems. Some other elements are present in far smaller amounts but are also part of many vital compounds; these are calcium, phosphorus, sulfur, potassium, chlorine, sodium and magnesium. Some of the remaining elements, such as copper and iron, are present only in tiny amounts but are nonetheless vital to our survival. For example, every molecule of haemoglobin, a compound in our red blood cells that carries oxygen around the body, contains a single atom of iron. In all, there are some 25 "essential elements" in our bodies.

The picture is similar for other life on Earth. Carbon, oxygen, hydrogen and nitrogen make up about 96 percent of the human body by mass, and for an *E. coli* bacterium it is about 91 percent, with smaller amounts of the other "essential elements." (In plants, the breakdown is similar, though some plant tissues also contain a small but significant amount of silicon which, after oxygen, is the most abundant element in rocky materials.) For life as we know it to have come into being, early Earth must have had a supply of these elements, and conditions that were conducive for them to come together to form a range of compounds.

Water vapor, nitrogen, and carbon dioxide—between them providing all four of the crucial elements of organic chemistry—made up most of the atmosphere on Earth as the

Above *Organic material, from beans to human beings, is composed almost entirely of carbon, oxygen, hydrogen, and nitrogen.*

Hadean Era came to an end. There was also liquid water on the surface, and the volatile nature of the planet—perturbed by large-scale shocks from volcanic activity, meteorite strikes, and lightning, created the right conditions to facilitate chemical reactions and allow the genesis of organic molecules.

Opposite *Sodium, most familiar to us in the form of the compound sodium chloride, has many important functions in living tissues.*

Composition of Earth's atmosphere over time

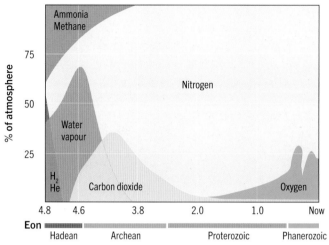

% of atmosphere (y-axis)

75
50
25

Ammonia
Methane
Nitrogen
Water vapour
H_2
He
Carbon dioxide
Oxygen

4.8   4.6   3.8   2.0   1.0   Now

Eon
Hadean   Archean   Proterozoic   Phanerozoic

Time (Giga annum (Ga)) billion years

ABIOGENESIS

The concept of life arising from non-living matter is called "abiogenesis." Many lab experiments have been carried out to try to replicate likely conditions on early Earth. They confirm that applying energy to the cocktail of compounds that would have been present in the atmosphere and the oceans would have generated a range of organic molecules, including sugars, and the various nucleotides that make up RNA and DNA. It is also possible that some of those first building blocks for life had an extra-terrestrial origin, as organic compounds composed of carbon and hydrogen are present in large quantities in space and have been found within meteorites.

// RNA World

Life as we know it is founded on RNA, and its sister molecule, DNA. Those familiar initials stand for ribonucleic acid and deoxyribonucleic acid respectively. Both of these two nucleic acids are present in all living things and have vital functions, providing the instructions and means by which an organism's body is built. We know that early Earth conditions could have generated the nucleotides from which nucleic acids are formed, from the various simpler chemicals that would have been present in the atmosphere and in surface water. These free nucleotides would naturally bond together to form pairs and chains—RNA molecules. The concept of "RNA World" posits a stage of pre-life development wherein abundant RNA molecules formed and self-replicated on early Earth, in water or on land that was periodically underwater and then dried out.

RNA is comprised of nucleotides—molecules that consist of a sugar called ribose, bonded to a nitrogenous base. Each nucleotide can bond to another via its ribose part, and RNA is a single spiral-shaped strand of nucleotides with the connected ribose elements forming its "backbone." There are four different types of nucleotides found in RNA, distinguished by the structure of the nitrogenous base

element—the types are adenine, cytosine, guanine and uracil. DNA is distinct from RNA in that it forms a double-stranded structure, with each nucleotide bonded to another on the opposite strand. This makes it more chemically stable than RNA. It is also formed of four types of nucleotides, and these are the same as in RNA except for uracil, which in DNA is replaced with the slightly different thymine.

In living cells, RNA's functions are primarily involved with building proteins. The "instructions" for this are held in the cell's DNA, and when a new protein needs to be synthesized, an RNA molecule is built that holds a copy of the relevant part of the DNA coding. These "messenger RNA" molecules travel to structures called ribosomes, which follow the copied code to assemble the required proteins, by combining amino acids (brought to them by "transport RNA") in the correct order. The ribosomes themselves are formed of a third kind of RNA—"ribosomal RNA."

RNA World proposes that some of the naturally formed RNA strands could have been able to successfully replicate themselves. This ability would have caused them to proliferate, and to potentially compete with one another, as there would likely have been differences in how stable

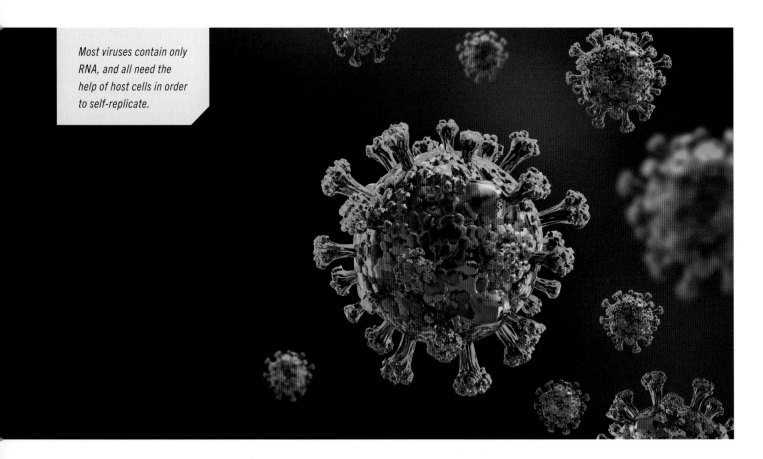

Most viruses contain only RNA, and all need the help of host cells in order to self-replicate.

different combinations of nucleotides were, and how readily, quickly, and efficiently they would be able to replicate themselves. Another theory suggests that RNA molecules could have evolved in concert with simple protein chains (peptides), which influenced the RNA molecules' replication.

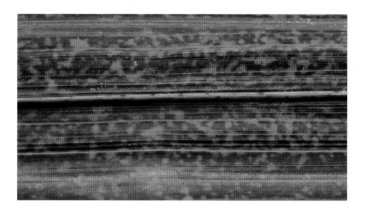

Above *Discoloration on a coconut palm leaf, caused by viroid infection.*

VIRUSES AND VIROIDS

Most viruses consist of a strand of RNA inside a protein coat. They invade cells (bacterial or more complex) and hijack the cell's own replication machinery to reproduce themselves. Even simpler than viruses are viroids, which are short, circular strands of RNA with no containing coat. Viroids reproduce themselves in a similar way, although they only affect the cells of flowering plants. They are the closest modern candidates for what the entities of RNA World may have looked and behaved like, although they are not free-living but rely on their much more complex hosts. Both viruses and viroids are not considered truly 'alive' but share some of the properties of unambiguously living things.

Below *Most viruses contain only RNA, and all need the help of host cells in order to self-replicate.*

Chemical structure of RNA and DNA

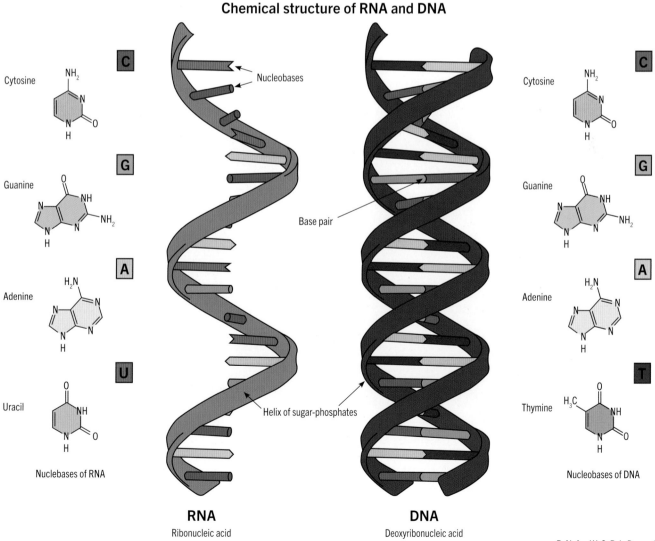

Cytosine **C**

Guanine **G**

Adenine **A**

Uracil **U**

Nuclebases of RNA

Nucleobases

Base pair

Helix of sugar-phosphates

Cytosine **C**

Guanine **G**

Adenine **A**

Thymine **T**

Nucleobases of DNA

RNA
Ribonucleic acid

DNA
Deoxyribonucleic acid

// The first living organisms

The earliest truly living things on Earth were simple single-celled prokaryotic organisms. The term "prokaryote" describes organisms whose cells are very small and do not contain a nucleus or other microstructures (organelles). Our own cells, along with those of other animals, as well as plants, fungi, and many single-celled organisms, are larger and contain organelles. Organisms with cells of this type are called eukaryotes. Life on Earth is generally classified into three domains—Archaea, Bacteria and Eukarya—and the first two of these comprise only prokaryotes. However, prokaryotes do fulfil all the criteria that define a living organism. They carry a genetic code in the form of DNA and, unlike viruses, they can self-replicate independently.

We know that prokaryotes existed at least 3.42 billion years ago, thanks to the discovery of microfossils in rock formations of this age, in what is now Western Australia. These fossils include representatives of both Bacteria and Archaea, and chemical evidence indicates that some of them produced methane while others consumed it, and some performed photosynthesis. Probable fossilized traces of prokaryotic life have also been found in 3.7 billion-year-old rock formations in Greenland, in the form of layers

Above *The molecular clock suggests that the most recent common ancestor of these two goose species lived about 9.5 million years ago—but they are still similar enough that they sometimes pair up and breed together.*

Below *Stromatolites in Australia, carrying microfossils of some of Earth's earliest life.*

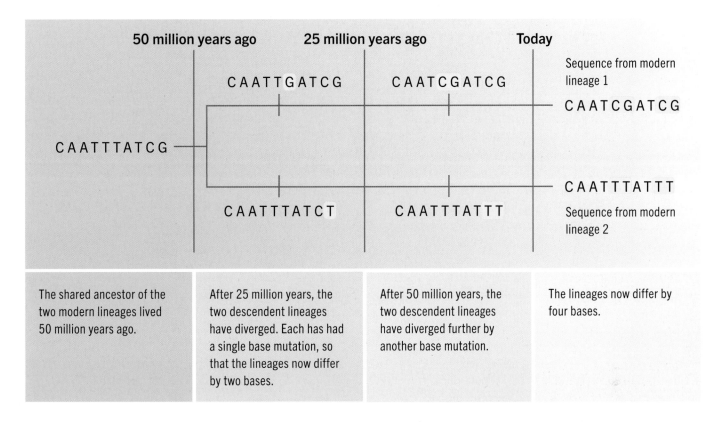

50 million years ago	25 million years ago	Today

CAATTGATCG → CAATCGATCG

Sequence from modern lineage 1

CAATCGATCG

CAATTTATCG

CAATTTATCT → CAATTTATTT

CAATTTATTT

Sequence from modern lineage 2

The shared ancestor of the two modern lineages lived 50 million years ago.	After 25 million years, the two descendent lineages have diverged. Each has had a single base mutation, so that the lineages now differ by two bases.	After 50 million years, the two descendent lineages have diverged further by another base mutation.	The lineages now differ by four bases.

Above *By comparing the DNA sequences of two related species, and applying our knowledge of the mutation rate, we can determine roughly how long ago their most recent shared ancestor would have lived.*

of sediment typical of the "microbial mats" produced by colonies of photosynthesizing cyanobacteria.

The Australian find in particular paints a picture of a well-established, diverse. and interdependent community of micro-organisms, suggesting a considerably earlier date for the actual first origin of life. Fossilized remains or traces of such tiny and delicate things are hard to find and to interpret, but analyzing fossils is not our only way to investigate early life on Earth. Enter the science of computer modeling, and the use of the "molecular clock." This method takes as its starting point the premise that life on Earth has developed like a branching tree. All forms descend from a single common ancestor, and lineages diverge over time through natural selection acting upon genetic variation generated by genetic mutations—the process of evolution. Once we know the rate at which genes tend to mutate, we can calculate how many "mutations ago" the shared common ancestor of any two organisms existed, by looking at differences in their DNA.

Molecular clock models set the likely date of the origin of life on Earth far further back—more than 4 billion years ago, and in some cases as early as 4.5 billion years ago. That life could have appeared so quickly after the planet's formation begs the question of whether its emergence was closer to an inevitability than a lucky fluke. Prokaryotes have continued to exist in great abundance on Earth ever since, and continue to vastly outnumber (and vastly influence) the more complex life that exists in our biosphere.

// Oxygenating the Earth

We need to breathe atmospheric oxygen to live—without it, we die in a matter of minutes. Some of our fellow animals can survive much longer without it, and many are able to extract it from water rather than air, but our metabolic processes all depend on its availability. It is therefore hard for us to conceive of life surviving and thriving without oxygen, but the first life on Earth did evolve in a world whose atmosphere and oceans were virtually oxygen-free.

The chemical reaction of respiration, by which a living cell releases energy from stored glucose, can occur with oxygen (aerobic respiration) or without it (anaerobic respiration). Our own cells are capable of both, but aerobic respiration generates far more energy, as well as producing more manageable by-products (water and carbon dioxide, which we can exhale, rather than lactic acid, which needs to be broken down in our livers). Some other anaerobic organisms produce different by-products—for example, yeasts generate ethanol alcohol through their respiration process.

Oxygen is dangerous to us and other modern organisms when it is in too-high concentrations. Modern Earth's atmosphere is about 21 percent oxygen. We struggle if it drops below 19 percent, but concentrations higher than 23.5 percent are also considered hazardous. Oxygen readily combines with other elements to form a great variety of compounds. This is why it is found so widely in our biochemistry, and why even small amounts of oxygen would have been so harmful to early-Earth organisms with a different biochemistry.

We know that photosynthesizing cyanobacteria, members of the domain Bacteria, existed at least 3.42 billion years ago. These organisms use light to drive a reaction that forms glucose molecules from carbon dioxide and water, and the by-product of this reaction is oxygen. It is likely that, initially, most of this oxygen quickly reacted with iron that was dissolved in the water, forming iron oxide—ancient rocks show vast deposits of the compound. However, at some point in the early history of life on Earth, the amount of oxygen generated by photosynthesizing cyanobacteria exceeded that which could be captured by dissolved iron. The result was a complete transformation of the atmosphere and the waters of the Earth, from almost oxygen-free to very oxygen-rich. This occurred sometime between 2.4 and 2 billion years ago and is known as the 'Great Oxidation Event'.

THE FIRST MASS EXTINCTION

There are numerous chemical markers found in ancient rocks that indicate that a sudden rise of oxygen levels took place. What we cannot see, but can certainly infer, is the impact that the Great Oxidation Event would have had on life on Earth. Oxygen poisoning would have caused massive die-offs, including among the cyanobacteria themselves. However, the extremely rapid reproductive cycles of many prokaryotes mean that evolutionary adaptation is also a rapid process. Those individual cells with a fortuitous resistance to oxygen poisoning—perhaps through genetic mutations that altered existing enzymes into new forms capable of denaturing oxygen—would have survived and proliferated in an environment suddenly free of highly competitive pressure. In the wake of this mass extinction, a new global environment was formed and new ways of life became possible.

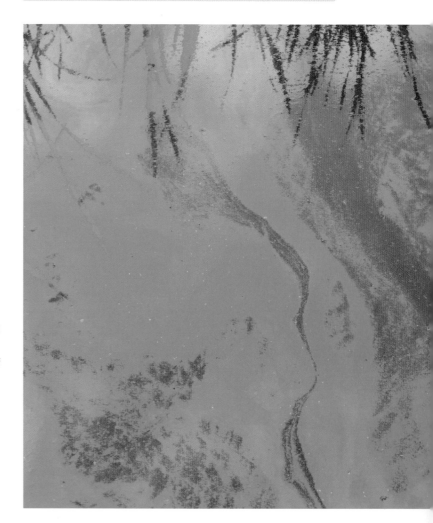

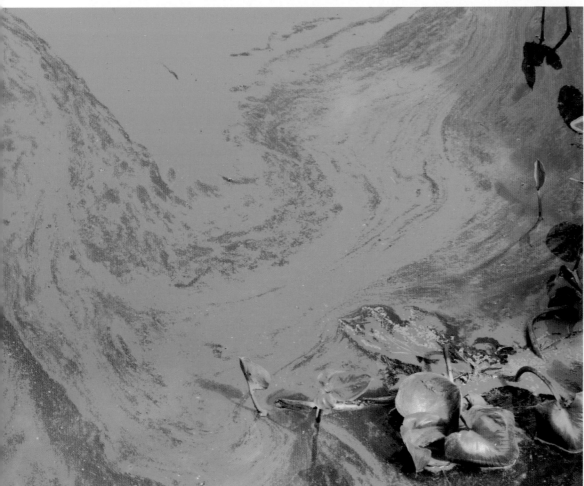

Above *We have harnessed the metabolic activity of micro-organisms in a variety of industries, including brewing.*

Left *Photosynthesis began with water-living micro-organisms, and their descendants are still the most significant suppliers of atmospheric oxygen.*

// The origin of eukaryotes

For many millions of years, Earth was full of life, but time-traveling humans may not have recognized it as such. Prokaryotes of many different kinds were the only life on our world for about 1.5 billion years—to put that enormous number into some context, the very first vertebrates on Earth only appeared some 500–600 million years ago, and mammals have only been around for about 178 million years. Our own species has existed for no more than 350,000 years. Nor is the age of the prokaryotes over, by any means—they are still vastly more abundant than eukaryotes and are much better placed to survive future mass extinctions.

Eukaryotes—organisms with complex cells, containing various organelles—descend from prokaryotes. The most obvious evidence of this comes courtesy of one of the most distinctive and vital types of organelle found in eukaryotic cells—the mitochondria. An individual mitochondrion bears a close resemblance to a bacterial cell in size, shape, and structure, and mitochondria also contain their own DNA, distinct from the cell's own DNA. Their function within the cell is to carry out aerobic respiration and thus provide the cell with its energy source. Within plant cells, there are also photosynthesizing organelles known as chloroplasts, which are very similar to free-living cyanobacteria.

Eukaryotic life therefore began as a symbiosis between different prokaryotes. The most accepted theory of exactly how this came about is that early Archaea engulfed early Bacteria, as modern eukaryotes are more similar to modern Archaea than they are to Bacteria, while the mitochondria and chloroplasts within eukaryotes are more similar to modern Bacteria. This theory would also arguably place Eukaryota as a subgroup of the domain Archaea, rather than a domain in its own right. The oldest clear evidence we have of eukaryotic life dates back at least 2.2 million years, possibly pre-dating the Great Oxidation Event.

A NOTE ABOUT CLASSIFICATION

Correctly categorizing living things is a powerful human motivator, but our criteria have evolved over time. In our early days as a species, we needed to group living things by whether they were edible or inedible, and harmless or dangerous. As our society progressed and our interest became more academic, we began to classify organisms according to their similarities in appearance and habits. Once the theory of evolution gained wide acceptance, we understood that all life has a common origin and that, through evolution, lineages diverge through time like the branches of a tree. Our classification systems (known as taxonomy) now sought to reflect the evolutionary history of different organisms and lineages of organisms. With the advent of genetic biology, we can now plot these family trees with much higher accuracy.

Today, the discipline of taxonomy is fast-moving and draws on many other different sciences, from anatomy and genetics to biochemistry and geology, to refine and correct our picture of how and when all life on Earth evolved. This can mean a headache for the layperson, as systems of classification are constantly changing and being updated. We must also allow for the fact that any evolutionary divergence of one lineage into two is a very gradual process, so no system of orderly 'boxes' will work perfectly to capture the messy reality of life.

Endosymbiosis

Ancestral prokaryote · Infolding of plasma membrane · Endosymbiosis · Ancestral photosynthesizing eukaryote

Above *The hot springs of Yellowstone Park are home to extremophile Archaea and Bacteria.*

Below *The origin of the fundamental branches of life's evolutionary tree.*

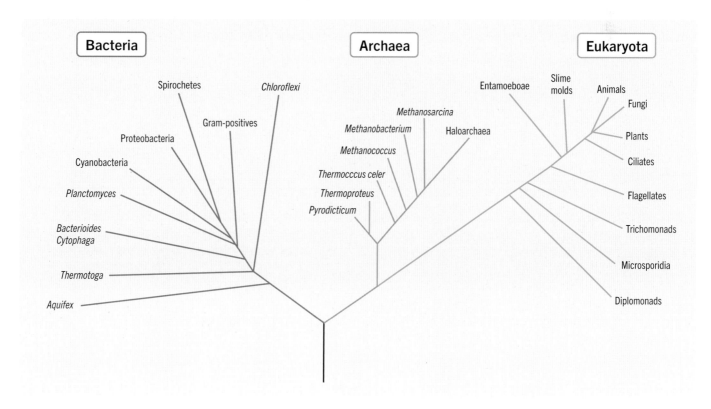

// Multicellularity

Those early eukaryotes were single-celled organisms, albeit much more complex cells than their prokaryote progenitors. Single-celled eukaryotes are still widespread on Earth today, and include groups such as *Euglena*, observed by many a young biology student having their first look through a microscope. An individual *Euglena* may be only one cell, 0.05 mm long, but it is nonetheless a complete and successful self-contained organism, equipped with chloroplasts to harness the Sun's energy, a beating flagellum to propel it through the water, a nucleus containing all of its genetic coding and the means to replicate itself, and many other tiny systems.

However, even the very earliest eukaryotes existed as multicellular organisms. In fact, multicellular communities can occur in prokaryotes too, with cyanobacterial cells known to form colonies, and bacteria of the group Myxococcota capable of forming moving aggregations and assembling into spore-producing structures. The benefits of multicellularity are quite intuitive to us as a social species—groups that work together can accomplish things that are out of reach for individuals. Within a multicellular community, different cells or groups of cells can handle different functions, and through evolution they can become more differentiated and specialized, and better at executing their particular tasks.

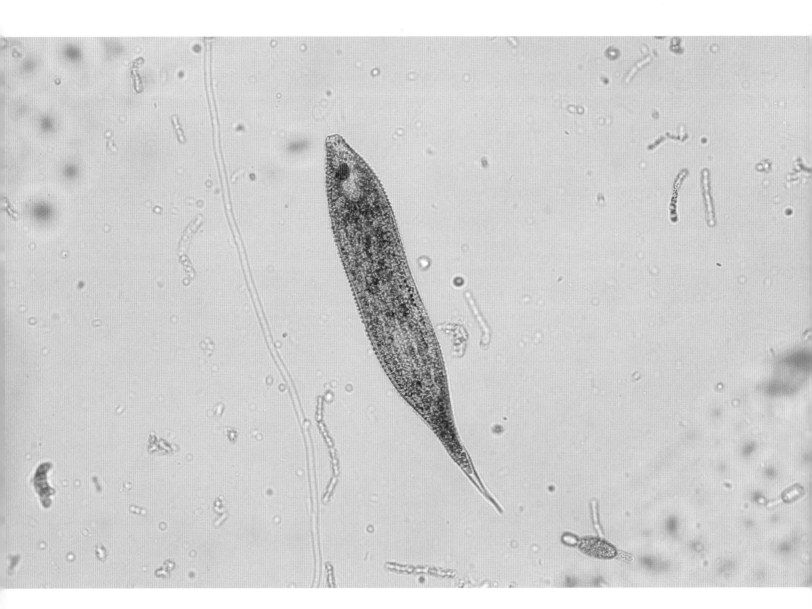

Above *Although it is a single-celled organism, this euglenid is many orders of magnitude more complex than any prokaryote.*

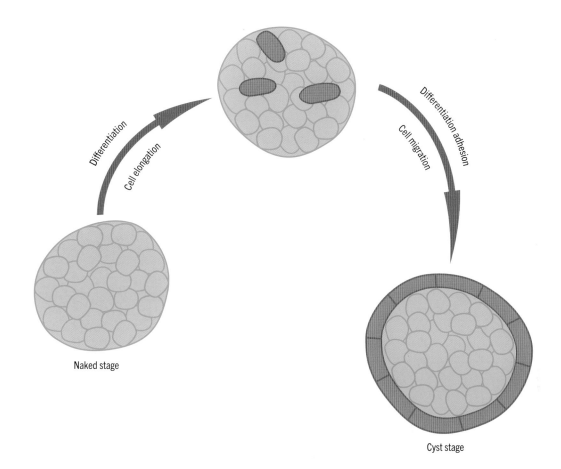

Naked stage

Cyst stage

There is evidence that multicellular life has evolved independently several times, in different groups of eukaryotes. Plants, fungi and animals all have an independent origin of multicellularity (in fact, it has evolved independently multiple times in plants and fungi). Nor has the direction of change been one-way—some lineages of multicellular organisms have descendants with reduced cell counts, some even becoming single-celled again.

Fossils of 2.4-billion-year-old fungal mycelia, found in South Africa in rock that made up part of the deep-sea biosphere, represent the earliest known multicellular eukaryote life. A microscopic fossil called *Bicellum*, found in 1-billion-year-old rocks in Scotland, is considered by some scientists to represent the earliest known multicellular animal, with a structure showing cells of two clearly differentiated types. There is also fossil evidence that multicellular early plants (algae) existed at least a billion years ago. The earliest ever multicellular land eukaryote found to date is the billion-year-old fungus *Ourasphaira giraldae.* Its fossilized remains were discovered in arctic Canada, and it long pre-dates the earliest land animals and plants.

Above *The organism* Bicellum *goes through a life stage in which it has two clearly differentiated cell types.*

FROM ONE TO MANY

The differences between a *Euglena* and an elephant, or even a *Euglena* and an earthworm, seem immense, and the leap from single-celled to multiple-celled life just as immense. However, in its simplest form, multicellularity is just two or more cells that remain stuck together. When one single-celled organism divides, the two daughter cells go their separate ways, but a single genetic mutation that affects the 'stickiness' of the cell membrane could mean that the two do not fully separate. The potential is then there for the two to share nutrients, to communicate information, or to join forces and move as one. In a cluster of cells, those on the outside will be better placed to interact with the environment (for example by gathering food, offloading waste products, and sensing danger) while those nearer the center, surrounded and protected by others, would be well placed to carry out metabolic processes (breaking down and storing food, building hormones and other useful molecules). The selective pressure toward differentiation is there as soon as cells begin to clump together.

The advent of animals

The three most familiar divisions or kingdoms of eukaryotes are plants, fungi and animals. Their precise taxonomy is somewhat more complex than this, but for the best part of 1 billion years these three well-differentiated groups have made up the vast majority of non-microscopic life on our planet. Today, animals contribute just 0.47 percent of the biomass (defined as the weight of carbon held in living biological entities) of all life on Earth, being significantly outweighed by fungi (2.2 percent), and vastly by plants (82.4 percent). The remainder of our planet's biomass is split between bacteria (12.8 percent), archaea (1.3 percent), protists, comprising most single-celled eukaryotes (0.7 percent) and viruses (0.04 percent, although by population they outnumber all other groups)!

As we saw previously, the first organism classed within the lineage of true animals was living about a billion years ago—*Bicellum*, so called because of its two cell types. There can be little doubt that many other early animals existed at that time or soon after, all originating as colonies of single-celled eukaryotes whose cell populations gradually differentiated. Over the next 600 million years, animal life proliferated and evolved in the world's oceans, though countless lineages are now long extinct. Of the animals we know today, the first ancestors of the animals known as sponges appear in the fossil record from 700 MYA, with some more controversial fossil evidence of an origin as early as 890 MYA. However, there is DNA evidence to suggest that another group, the ctenophores or comb jellies, was the first modern animal lineage to emerge.

Sponges and ctenophores are very different. The former are non-moving or sessile, almost plant-like, and may grow to a great size. Their porous structure allows sea water to flow through them, and specialized cells on their outer surfaces capture nutrient particles from the water as it passes. Ctenophores are small jelly-like, globular animals, bearing rows of beating cilia on their bodies that propel them though the water (the resultant hairy appearance has earned them the nickname of "sea gooseberries"). Modern ctenophores are active predators, many possessing a pair of long tentacles to ensnare prey.

There are at least 3 million and possibly as many as 30 million animal species on Earth today. Our planet's animal population may be miniscule in biomass terms, but animals have had a disproportionate influence on the course of all life on Earth. One animal species in particular has proved so

Below *Ctenophores or comb jellies may have been the first true animals to evolve on Earth.*

successful that it now contributes a hefty 2.2 percent of all animal biomass, while the handful of other species that it farms for its own use make up 3.9 percent. Yet many millions of other animal species evolved, thrived, and became extinct for hundreds of millions of years before anything resembling a human being ever walked on the Earth.

MUSHROOM COUSINS

When we observe the natural world, many of us make a lot of assumptions and inferences, and these inform the way we categorize life in our own minds. Most of us value ourselves and each other above other living things, so we see human traits as representing the pinnacle of evolution (though also offering grudging admiration to those species that have an exceptional specific skill that's relevant to our own interests, such as running very fast). Living things that don't (visibly) move, let alone think and talk, are at the bottom of the heap, and although we recognize the oxygen-giving value of plants, when it comes to fungi, we are deeply unimpressed. We tend to class them as a less useful and less decorative form of plant. However, fungal cell biology reveals that these life forms share a more recent common ancestor with animals, not plants. The button mushrooms in the supermarket may sit next to the onions, but they are in fact more closely related to you than they are to any onion!

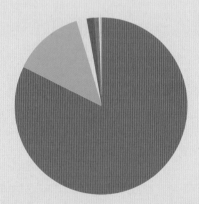

Taxon	Mass (Gt C)	% of total
Plants	450	82.4%
Bacteria	70	12.8%
Fungi	12	2.2%
Archaea	7	1.3%
Protists	4	0.70%
Animals	2.589	0.47%
Viruses	0.2	0.04%

Above *A breakdown of Earth's total biomass, by organism type.*

Below *They resemble bizarre underwater plants, but the structure of their cells reveals that sponges are animals.*

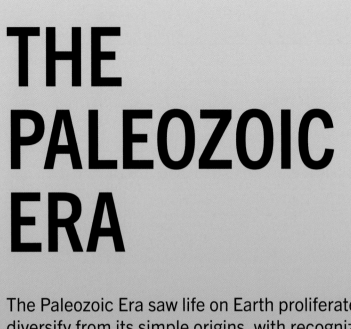

THE PALEOZOIC ERA

The Paleozoic Era saw life on Earth proliferate and diversify from its simple origins, with recognizable ancestors of many of today's familiar species making their first appearances. While complex invertebrate life thrived in the oceans, some animals and plants left the water, evolving anatomical and physiological traits that allowed them to tolerate life in the open air. The first great forests spread across the land, and super-sized insects shared this new habitat with early vertebrates. The era also saw climatic and tectonic shifts and seismic activity, and the reconfiguration of Earth's lands and seas eventually brought about the most devastating mass extinction of the planet's history.

Trilobite fossils. One of the earliest arthropod groups, trilobites were one of the most successful of all animal groups, existing in the oceans for more than 270 million years.

// Overview of the era

The Paleozoic Era, the first of three eras in our current (Phanerozoic) geological eon, began around 541 MYA and ended 251.9 MYA. This 289-million-year span saw our planet go through dramatic geological change and also saw the rise (and in many cases, fall) of a vast array of increasingly complex life, including the first land-dwelling vertebrates. In particular, this era is characterized by a relatively rapid and expansive diversification of animal life at its beginning, the rise and global spread of land plants, and then the most cataclysmic ever mass extinction (so far) at its end.

The era is divided into six periods, beginning with the Cambrian (541–485 MYA). This was followed by the Ordovician (485–443 MYA), the Silurian (443–419 MYA), the Devonian (419–359 MYA), and the Carboniferous (subdivided into the Mississippian and Pennsylvanian) (359–299 MYA). The final period in the era was the Permian, which began 299 MYA and ended 252 MYA.

Continental drift through the Paleozoic saw the landmasses of the Earth move apart, breaking up what was probably a supercontinent (known as Rodinia). They then gradually came together again to form the supercontinent Pangaea by the end, with the formation of tremendous mountain ranges where land masses borne on moving continental plates collided with one another. The early part of the era also saw a warming climate and rises in sea levels, followed by a significant ice age in the late Ordovician. The Carboniferous Period was characterized by repeated ice ages, brought about by atmospheric changes as living organisms spread on the land. These changes to geography and climate strongly influenced the way living things evolved and where and when they colonized different parts of the world, and also strongly tested their powers of adaptation.

The fossil record from this era becomes vastly more informative than that of earlier times. Large numbers of exquisitely detailed fossils have been found from the Cambrian Period onwards. Many of these are unmistakably ancient members of lineages that survive today, while others are like nothing at all from the modern world and defy confident classification even today.

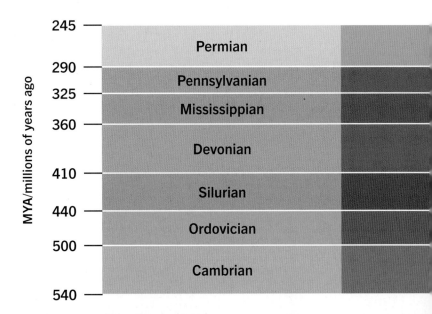

MYA/millions of years ago

245 — Permian
290 — Pennsylvanian
325 — Mississippian
360 — Devonian
410 — Silurian
440 — Ordovician
500 — Cambrian
540 —

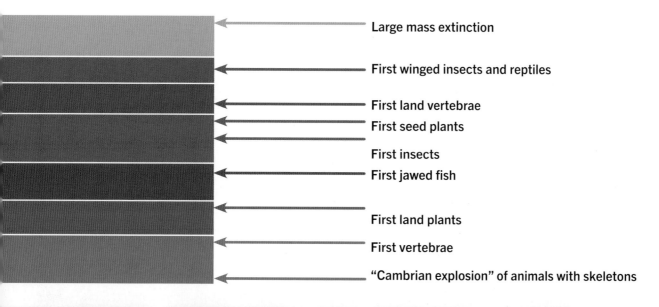

Large mass extinction

First winged insects and reptiles

First land vertebrae

First seed plants

First insects

First jawed fish

First land plants

First vertebrae

"Cambrian explosion" of animals with skeletons

Above *Evolutionary timeline of the Paleozoic Era.*

Left *The Carboniferous is noted for its extensive, lush forests, creating a high-oxygen atmosphere that supported a range of super-sized land invertebrates.*

Geographical flux

The familiar configuration of the world's land masses today will remain unchanged throughout our lifetime, to our eyes at least. However, movement and change is continuous. Computer simulations that cram Earth's 4.5-billion-year geological history into a few minutes show how those familiar continental shapes rise from the seas, grow and shrink, turn and tilt, and glide across the oceans, coming together and parting again and again. It is also possible to predict and model how the continents will change over the remaining lifespan of our Earth. This is continental drift, and its existence has only been accepted by mainstream science since the early 20th century.

It is not just the continents that move but the entire lithosphere of our planet—the rocky material forming the crust and the very top of the mantle below, which sits atop the hotter and more freely moving layers of mantle closer to the center of the Earth. The lithosphere is formed of several pieces or plates, each of which carries continental and ocean-holding parts. Over their slow journeys, plates may fuse or fracture, but some are much more stable and ancient than others. Their geography and geology, and the mechanics of their movement, form the science of plate tectonics.

Through the Paleozoic Era, continental drift and the influence of our world's abundance of living creatures both exerted critical influences on the course of evolution. The process of evolution shapes living things to be better adapted to their environment, but if an environment is constantly changing, all the features that make an organism the "best-

adapted" will also change. An animal that survives well through an ice age will not fare so well in a period of global warming. This is selective pressure, and it is the key driver of evolutionary change. Natural selection, the process that removes the "worst-adapted" individuals from the population, is also the cause of extinctions, because sometimes even the "best-adapted" is not good enough. In periods of relatively rapid geological and climate change, as occurred at several key points through the Paleozoic Era, extinctions came thick and fast because evolutionary change did not keep pace with environmental change.

Plate tectonics and climate variation reshape the land and seas in a huge variety of ways. When plates meet, mountains can form on land and below the sea, and when they separate, they form rifts. The boundaries between plates are hotspots for earthquakes, and volcanoes also tend to form in these areas. The destruction wrought by major earthquakes and volcanic eruptions is obviously devastating to whatever life is present in the immediate vicinity at the time, but the remodeled landscape can provide opportunities for newly colonizing life forms. Similarly, when the Earth's continents come together, the center of a supercontinent's vast land mass can suffer more extreme weather, especially drought. The length of coastline and extent of shallow sea is also much reduced, and changes in climate also affect sea levels, with consequences for marine life.

Below *The earth's tectonic plates.*

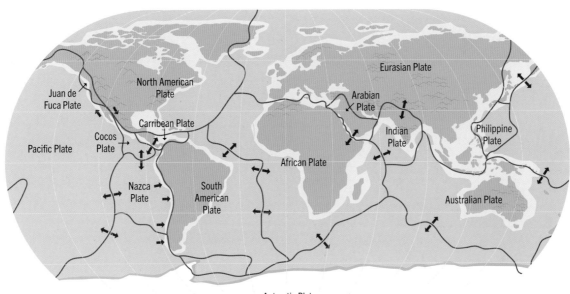

The East African Rift System marks an area of ongoing tectonic activity.

// The Cambrian explosion

The fossil record provides us with evidence that complex marine life took off in a very big way in the Cambrian Period. Most of the animal phyla (a phylum is a lineage just below the Kingdom level in taxonomy) that are still with us today had their advent in Cambrian times, as did many more that have not survived to the present day. Many of the Cambrian fossils that we marvel over are exceptionally well preserved and detailed, thanks partially to the hard body parts of the animals that left them.

Hard body parts, made largely from calcium carbonate, break down very slowly after the animal's death compared to soft tissues. When this happens in slow-settling sediment, beautiful fossil imprints can form in the resultant sedimentary rock. We might wonder, therefore, whether life was just as abundant and diverse before the Cambrian explosion, but simply not preserved for our gaze due to the fact that animals living prior to this did not have hard body parts. The evidence that there was indeed a relatively sudden radiation of new life forms includes the existence of the "SSF" or "small, shelly fauna" that existed prior to the Cambrian. These animals, the first bearers of calcium carbonate body parts, first appeared in the Ediacaran Period at the end of the Proterozoic Eon. Most of them are generally small, with apparently simple anatomy. One well-represented example, the genus *Cloudina*, left behind cup-shaped fossils, each a few millimetres long, in nested stacks that connected through holes at their bases. Nothing very meaningful can be inferred about the body shape and way of life of the animal or animals that lived inside the shell, and *Cloudina*'s classification, beyond it being an animal, is *incertae sedis*—a term that translates as "of uncertain placement."

There are some larger SSF animals, and some do not even have much in the way of shell. Their great diversity has led to some palaeontologists nicknaming them "small, silly fauna" instead, but they do appear to share the trait of simple anatomy and slow (or no) movement, and most are likely to have grazed on the

Above *Fossilized shells of the Cambrian animal* Cloudina.

abundance of algae and other single-celled life forms that formed "microbial mats" on underwater surfaces. Beyond the early Cambrian Period, though, SSF fossils are suddenly joined by more complex forms, whose hard preserved parts included not only detailed shells, but also limbs, sensory organs and feeding anatomy—in many cases their bodies indicated they had an active and fast-paced lifestyle. These new animals included early predators, whose evolution also

forced non-predatory animals along evolutionary pathways toward higher complexity, with natural selection favoring those better able to defend themselves. With growing complexity and diversity came new opportunities for animals to evolve into new ways of life.

Below *Fossils of micro-organisms, in the form of microbial mats, built up over millions of years to form stromatolites.*

A HELPING HAND FOR HUNTERS

As we have seen, rapid increases in oxygen levels early in life's history caused large-scale extinctions. However, by the early Cambrian, animals were well adapted to a more oxygenated environment. Oxygen levels continued to fluctuate, but the changes were much more moderate. We can infer this through study of the composition of sedimentary rocks that formed in those times. Metallic elements such as iron and molybdenum become more soluble in water as oxygen levels change, so their abundance in rock gives a good indication of how oxygen-rich the waters were when that rock was formed. A relatively modest rise in oxygen levels would have been enough to drive the evolution of early predators—we can infer this by looking at the life present on modern-day seabeds, as predators tend to be scarce or absent in oxygen-depleted environments.

Mysteries of the Burgess Shale

S ome of the most spectacular finds of Cambrian life came from the Burgess Shale, a 508-million-year-old deposit in the Canadian Rockies. The palaeontologist Charles Walcott and his family extracted more than 65,000 specimens from parts of this outcrop between 1910 and 1924, and tens of thousands more have been recovered since then. The finds included early representatives of many animal groups still living today, as well as other long-lost lineages, several of them so unusual that they have foxed scientists for decades.

The most iconic Burgess animal is probably the spine- and tentacle-bearing *Hallucigenia*. Its very name captures the bizarre nature of its appearance, and although it has left behind a good number of very clear and detailed fossils, so strange is its form that palaeontologists have long been unable to confidently classify it—or even which way up it may have oriented itself in the water, or whether it might have been a detached appendage from another larger animal, rather than a complete organism.

A similar confusion initially surrounded *Anomalocaris*, whose mouth, body, and feeding appendages were initially all regarded as whole, separate individual animals, before entire fossils were found. These revealed *Anomalocaris* to be a large, powerful and active predator, with huge eyes on stalks, a fearsome pair of segmented, curved structures for grasping food, and a wide, flattened body and tail that would have moved up and down to provide a dolphin-like swimming action.

Today, *Anomalocaris* is regarded as an early offshoot of the phylum Arthropoda, cousin to modern insects, crustaceans and other jointed-legged invertebrates. Some other Burgess oddities, such as the five-eyed *Opabinia* and the beautiful *Marella* or "lace crab," are also now classed as early arthropods whose lineages did not persist into modern times. Some finds have now been classified as representatives of other modern phyla, such as *Wiwaxia*, usually now regarded as a form of mollusc (though classed as a polychaete worm by some biologists) and *Pikaia*, a member of our own phylum (Chordata). *Hallucigenia* is now considered to belong to the phylum Lobopodia, whose modern members include the tardigrades.

STEMS AND CROWNS

All of the Burgess animals described here are examples of "stem group" members of their respective phyla. When a new lineage evolves, it generally undergoes adaptive radiation, diversifying and expanding into different available niches. Over time, some of these groups will prove the most successful in the long term and will continue to evolve, while others will fall by the wayside, eventually leaving a much smaller group of survivors after a long tract of evolutionary time. This can be visualized as a growing bush whose new branches are rigurously pruned, leaving just a few to continue to grow. Those members of the group that live in modern times, along with their direct shared ancestors, form the "crown group" of that lineage, while the early offshoots form the "stem group."

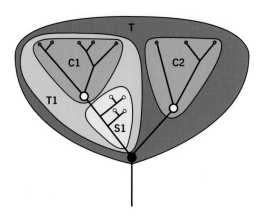

Above *Evolutionary tree showing the extant crown groups (C1 and C2) and an extinct stem group (S1) within total lineages (T and T1).*

Left *An undersea scene featuring various Cambrian animals, including the large predator* Anomalocaris *swimming over smaller* Opabinia, *with* Hallucigenia *walking on the rocky seabed.*

// Trilobites and ammonites

Some of the lineages that first emerged at or around the beginning of the Paleozoic Era thrived and prospered tremendously, becoming among the most diverse and abundant on the planet for many millions of years. Two of the most successful groups of this era, as evidenced by their abundant fossils, which are familiar to many of us, were the trilobites and ammonites.

Trilobites were arthropods, and many had a very generalized body plan compared to familiar modern arthropods such as beetles and bees, shrimps, spiders, and scorpions. The body is oval in shape, with two wide lobes either side of a narrower central one—(hence "trilobite"—three-lobed). It is segmented, with all segments being about the same width. Each segment has a branched appendage on each side—one branch functions as a leg and the other as a gill. The head or cephalon bears a pair of antennae, eyes, and a simple mouth. Beyond these basic features, trilobite body forms varied considerably. Some were streamlined or even winged swimmers, while others crawled on the seabed or buried themselves in the substrate. Some were eye-less deep-water filter-feeders, while others were active hunters with large eyes and, in some cases, strong legs with which they wrestled and crushed their prey.

Ammonite fossils, with their ridged coil of shell, remind us of modern-day snails. They were indeed molluscs, in the same phylum as snails, but were closer cousins to today's squids and octopuses. The shell was divided inside by walls or septa, into a series of chambers—as the animal grew, it formed and moved into a new chamber, leaving the previous one empty. A similar structure and growth pattern can be seen in the modern-day nautiluses. The ammonites were soft-bodied, had eyes, and were able to swim. They extended their tentacles into the water to feed—in most cases on plankton, but the largest species could have captured bigger prey.

Trilobites pre-date the Cambrian, although this period saw their greatest diversity. The last trilobites survived until the end of the Paleozoic Era. Ammonites appeared on the scene rather later, with the earliest fossils dating back to the Devonian Period, midway through the Paleozoic. The last survivors made it all the way to the mass extinction at the end of the Cretaceous Period.

Left *Trilobites, a group of early arthropods, lived through the Paleozoic Era and have left behind numerous beautiful fossils.*

FOSSIL HUNTING

There are many sites around the world with rich fossil deposits, and at some of these there is unrestricted access for you to search for fossil finds of your own. Famous sites include Lyme Regis in Dorset, UK, and Penn Dixie Fossil Park & Nature Reserve in New York state, USA. With a few simple tools, you can carefully break pieces of sedimentary rock and see what is hidden within. Ammonites and trilobites are among the likeliest finds, as are shark teeth (since sharks, both ancient and modern, shed many teeth through their long lifespans). Always take safety precautions, for example wearing safety goggles when breaking rocks, monitoring the tide at coastal sites, and being mindful of the chance of rock falls. Some sites have their own code of conduct regarding how many specimens to take. Even where collection is unlimited, it is good practice to notify registered local museums if you find something unusual, so that it can be properly documented.

// The first chordates

As we have seen, among the animals found in the Burgess Shale deposits, dating back to the mid-Cambrian Era, was an early chordate, named *Pikaia*. This 5cm (2in)-long, simple-looking animal was, in some ways, less intriguing at first glance than many of the other Burgess oddities, being a slim, vertically flattened, leaf-shaped animal with no legs or fins, just a double row of gills at its front end, and a pair of feeding tentacles and some other shorter and simpler appendages on its rather tiny and indistinct head. However, compared to other more complex-looking animals alive at the time, *Pikaia* is closer to our own ancestral path.

Pikaia closely resembles a modern lineage of non-vertebrate chordates—the lancelets. These animals look like very 'stripped-down' fishes, with translucent skin revealing muscle segments along the length of the body, only a hint of a tail fin and no other fins at all, simple eyes, and a jaw-less mouth. Inside a lancelet you will find no bones, but a notochord—a central column of tough but flexible connective tissue. Notochords exist in all chordates at some point in their development, though in vertebrates they are replaced with a bony vertebral column during early development.

The chordates' closest modern relatives are the echinoderms (starfish, sea urchins, and related species) and the acorn worms (a small group of burrowing marine animals). Together, these animals plus chordates form the group known as deuterostomes. The earliest probable deuterostome fossil dates back to about 540 MYA, with the earliest chordate fossils dated at about 520 MYA. Molecular evidence also supports a relatively rapid divergence between chordates and other deuterostomes, but suggests that deuterostomes may have existed for much longer than the fossil record indicates—perhaps as long as 900 million years.

Above *Pikaia has a vaguely fishy form, and was one of the first ever chordates (the group within which the vertebrate animals arose).*

Below *Although they resemble sponges, the tunicates are more complex than they look, and are close cousins to the vertebrates.*

Pikaia and other early chordates were swimming animals, and probably filter-feeders. They would also have been hunted by larger animals, such as *Anomalocaris*. The need to escape these dangers would have placed selective pressure on them to become faster swimmers, or better at hiding, or more robust anatomically. The related acorn worms have followed the "better hiders" path, while the tunicates, a modern group of non-vertebrate chordates, are mostly non-moving and have an array of other ways to protect themselves.

TUNICATES

The tunicates or sea squirts are poorly represented in the fossil record, as they lack hard body parts, but have existed for at least 555 million years. The majority of these bizarre animals live attached to the seabed, look rather featureless and blob-like, and in short do not seem very like us at all. However, they are true chordates with complex internal anatomy. In their larval form, they are mobile and tadpole-like, and a few retain this form throughout their lives. Most, though, settle and fix onto the seabed (some in a colonial form), where they live by drawing in and squirting out sea water through a pair of siphons. Their body covering or tunic helps protect them from predators—it contains cellulose, a tough connective tissue that is extremely rare in animals but is found in most of the world's plant species.

The first marine plants

As we have seen, water-living cyanobacteria were the first organisms to develop the ability to photosynthesize. There is also evidence from 1.2 billion years ago that they were able to live on land at the water's edge, albeit much less prolifically than in the water itself. These simple prokaryotic life forms live on today in little-changed form, but they also have a lineage that took a very different path. Through endosymbiosis, they became chloroplasts—organelles that exist within the cells of plants, where they continue to capture the Sun's energy through photosynthesis.

The simplest plants living today are the green algae, and the first photosynthesizing eukaryotes would also be classed as green algae. Most species within this classification are single-celled organisms, although some form colonies, and others are multicellular with a range of differentiated cell types—those in the latter category are what we recognize today as green seaweeds. Their photosynthesis is carried out by the chloroplasts in their cells, which contain two types of chlorophyll pigment. When exposed to sunlight, the chlorophyll molecules absorb light of certain wavelengths, triggering a chemical reaction that results in the creation of glucose. Glucose molecules are combined to create starches—the cell's energy store. Wavelengths of visible green light are reflected by their chlorophyll, rather than absorbed, which is why these organisms (and most other plants) appear green to us.

Fossils of green algae exist from the Cambrian Period and perhaps earlier, although older fossils are more ambiguous and difficult to classify. The order Dasycladales is well represented in the fossil record because these algae secrete calcium carbonate, meaning they are more likely to be preserved. There are still living members of the order, but many more fossil genera have been found (from the Cambrian through to the end of the Cretaceous) than are living today. One living example, *Acetabularia*, is remarkable in that individuals can be up to 10cm (4in) long, but are still single-celled.

Above *Algae, such as this* Ulva, *lack the complex structure of familiar land plants, but they do have the vital ability to photosythesize.*

Opposite Acetabularia *is a single-celled green alga, with a stem-and-cap structure that recalls a land fungus.*

The genus *Botryococcus*, a single-celled colonial green alga, was very abundant from the Carboniferous onward and was a key contributor to the oil and coal deposits that we are using as fossil fuels today. The genus still exists, and the species *Botryococcus braunii* is being researched as a possible sustainable source of hydrocarbon oils.

THE FIRST LAND PLANT?

Land plants evolved from green algae living in fresh water, most likely from representatives of the orders Charales or Coleochaetales, both of which are multicellular forms that still exist today. The first land plants resembled modern liverworts. They were non-vascular plants (meaning they did not have vein-like systems for transporting water and nutrients), tiny in size and simple in anatomy, and reproduced by spores rather than forming seeds. These first simple land plants appeared 470 MYA or earlier, and would initially have been dependent on wet environments.

// Setting foot on land—breathing the air

Some 375 MYA, in what is now Arctic Canada, a curious fish (which today we call *Tiktaalik*) walked awkwardly out of the water on its sturdy lobe-shaped fins, took a breath of fresh air, and that was the beginning of vertebrate life on Earth. This pivotal (though imaginary) moment has been captured in many artists' impressions, but of course real-life evolution does not tend to proceed in pivotal moments. In any case, invertebrate animals of various kinds had already breathed air and colonized land millions of years before.

As much as we would struggle to adapt to a life in the water, so land represented a dangerous and hostile environment to animals whose evolutionary history was entirely aquatic. They had gills to extract oxygen from the water, body shapes adapted to move through water and be supported by it, their bodily waste would be quickly carried away by the water that surrounded them, and their internal water-filtering and balancing systems were of course quite different to anything that would work on land. However, the land and its burgeoning plant life offered opportunities for new ways of life for animals, and it was the already highly successful arthropods, equipped with legs to walk on the seabed, that were best placed to begin to exploit these opportunities.

One of the earliest known fossils of a land-dwelling arthropod is about 414 million years old. The animal in question, *Pneumodesmus newmani*, is classed as a

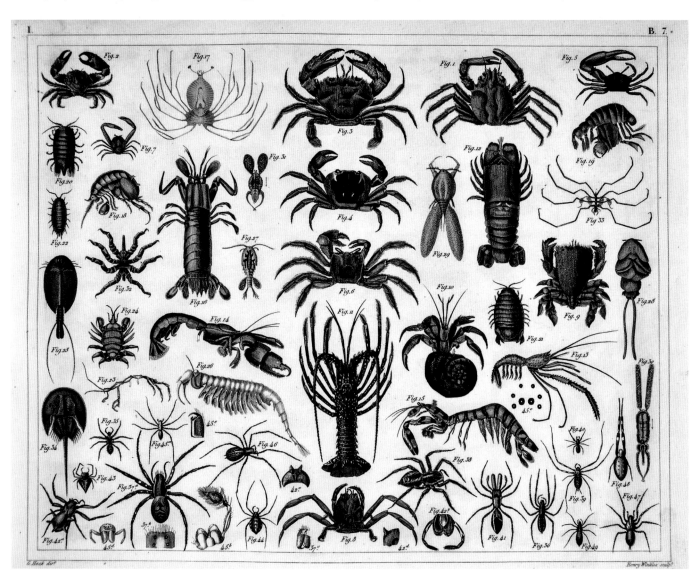

Above *This 1849 print depicts various groups of mainly marine arthropods, including crabs, shrimps, horseshoe crabs and sea spiders.*

myriapod—the arthropod grouping that includes centipedes and millipedes. Evidence of it being air-breathing comes courtesy of the spiracles on each of its body segments—openings to let air in and out. Another early air-breathing myriapod, *Kampecaris obanensis*, is even older—this 1.2 in (3 cm)-long animal lived in wet areas around lake shores some 425 MYA. The eurypterids, related to modern spiders and scorpions, were fearsome predators whose anatomy suggested an amphibious lifestyle.

Most modern crustaceans are aquatic, but some (such as woodlice and a few species of crabs) live entirely or mostly on land. Some can breathe underwater and on land, and show behavioral modifications to cope with the challenges of living in both environments. The first crustaceans to begin to transition to a life on land would have lived in environments that were underwater some of the time. The insects, most successful and diverse of all land animals, arose from one of these early crustacean lineages. Many modern insects no longer need any prolonged contact with a watery environment to survive, being fully air-breathing with body cuticles that resist dehydration and having evolved a range of ways to get around efficiently in a land-and-air environment—most notably, they were the first animal group to evolve the power of flight.

Above *Sandhoppers can be found in the intertidal zone—these tiny arthropods are comfortable in and out of water.*

GILLS AND TRACHEAE

As we have seen, the basic arthropod body plan includes a pair of gills on either side of each body segment, each gill being paired with a leg. Some stem arthropods, such as *Anomalocaris*, had a simpler system, and some modern arthropods also have a simplified body plan—for example insects have dispensed with their gills (in fact their wings are probably highly modified gills!) and most of their legs. Insects obtain oxygen from the air via spiracles—openings in their cuticles that lead to a system of tubes or tracheae in which gas exchange takes place. There is evidence from developmental studies of crustaceans and insects that tracheae and gills develop from the same original pathway. Some modern insects are wholly or partially aquatic and have evolved new ways to obtain oxygen from their environment—some have evolved new forms of gills, while others trap bubbles of air from the surface to serve as a sort of aqualung while they are underwater.

// Mosses, lichens, and fungi

From green algae came land plants, which were to remodel Earth's land surfaces completely and dramatically as the Paleozoic Era progressed. However, plants still had a long way to go before they would reach Carboniferous forest proportions. The first land plants, as we have seen, were non-vascular and are ancestral to modern liverworts. Liverworts and their ancestors, along with other non-vascular plants including hornworts and mosses, are known as bryophytes. Mosses first appear in the fossil record in the early stages of the Carboniferous Period, although they are poorly representedas fossils and may have existed earlier.

Mosses and liverworts grew then, as now, in dense mats that spread across the land, and their impact on the landscape of our world was profound. As the first land-living photosynthesizers present in any significant numbers, they boosted atmospheric oxygen levels to new highs, and their released carbon dioxide cooled down the planet. They eroded rock into soil, creating conditions that encouraged

Above *Non-vascular plants such as mosses and liverworts grow in profusion in damp and shady areas.*

the evolution of more complex plant life, and they provided food and habitat for early land animals. They reproduced by releasing spores, or asexually (with broken pieces able to form new plants).

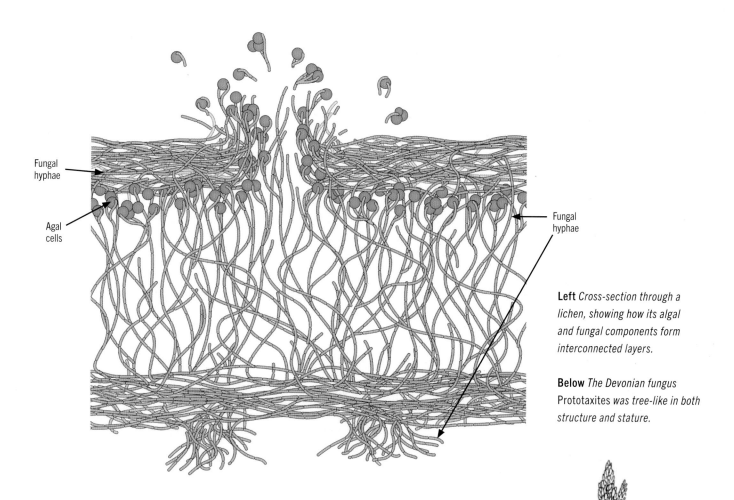

Fungal
hyphae

Agal
cells

Fungal
hyphae

Left *Cross-section through a lichen, showing how its algal and fungal components form interconnected layers.*

Below *The Devonian fungus* Prototaxites *was tree-like in both structure and stature.*

Lichens are often confused with mosses, as they tend to form mats on rocks and other surfaces, and can have a branching, plant-like structure. However, they are quite different biologically. A lichen is a composite organism, comprising an alga or cyanobacteria living in intimate association with a fungus. The plant element of the lichen is photosynthetic, while the fungus element anchors the lichen to a substrate and is also efficient at collecting water. The oldest known unambiguous fossil lichen, *Winfrenatia*, existed some 400 MYA, and although the group has a poor fossil record, it is widely accepted that lichens evolved later than the first land plants.

Fungi themselves were the first life forms to exist on land and, like mosses, were and still are important soil-forming organisms. Their presence helped the first land plants to spread away from the water's edge. Today we know that, because of their extensive network of underground fibers (mycelia), some individual fungi could be defined as the largest living things in existence. However, in the Devonian Period we would not have had to go digging into the earth to find gigantic fungi. Before the evolution of trees, this landscape was punctuated by "mega fungi" such as *Prototaxites* that stood up to 26.2 ft (8 m) tall. They provided a food source for many early invertebrates, although different fungi lineages (at the opposite end of the size scale) were also evolving ways to infect and parasitize insects and other animals, as well as plants. In fact, the lichens, now incredibly intimate symbiotic associations of plant and fungus, may have originated through parasitic fungi attacking algae.

// Soil formation and early land ecosystems

S oil is vital for the rich diversity of life on land as we know it. In the sea, nutrients in the form of tiny bits of organic matter may collect as sediment in certain places on the seabed, but they are also suspended in the water, where they provide food for filter-feeding animals of all kinds, both immobile and swimming. On land, organic matter cannot easily hang in the air for any length of time so it accumulates on the ground as soil, especially in places that are naturally sheltered from the wind.

Right *The first land plants and fungi would have evolved around margins of lakes and other freshwater bodies.*

Below *The soil that builds up wherever plants grow is a rich and hugely important habitat.*

This organic matter enables plants to grow, as it holds water and nutrients that they can reach with their roots. Over time, a plant community erodes rock, creates sheltered conditions at ground level on its own, and also stabilizes the soil. This all encourages the accumulation of more soil. Soil, made primarily of particles of eroded rock along with organic materials (broken-down dead things and natural waste), is the essential foundation of land ecosystems and is home to an array of other living things besides the roots of the plant, from a vast community of bacteria to nematodes and earthworms, fungal mycelia, burrowing insects, and even tunnelling mammals that almost never emerge into the light. All of these have their role to play in modifying soil structure and composition.

In the early days of plants and fungi colonizing the land, soils would have first developed on the edges of bodies of water, where the movement of the water would have left organic material—animal waste and the remains of aquatic organisms that had died—on the shore from time to time. This added the potential for life support to any rock sediment already present. As the first land plants and fungi colonized these environments and began to create their own soil, their photosynthesizing activity cooled down the planet's atmosphere (because they removed carbon dioxide from the air), and increased glaciation meant increased erosion of rock—more sediment, and more soil. When larger plants with heftier root systems began to appear, they also reshaped the landscape by diverting and channeling fresh water into rivers.

The land animals at the time would have relied on the existence of soil to a greater or lesser extent. The first land arthropods would have been amphibious and able to return to the water to avoid their bodies becoming desiccated, and to seek food or shelter as necessary. Soil under plant growth, though, would remain damp and the air above humid enough to have helped these animals begin to adapt to living full time on the ground. Soil and the plants and fungi that grew in it also provided food sources. As these plant- and detritus-eating animals spread and diversified, so early predators began to emerge, hunting smaller animals.

// Bones and teeth—the first vertebrates

The chordates, as we have seen, were present in Cambrian times, in forms not too dissimilar from some of those living today. However, most modern chordates belong to the subphylum Vertebrata, and are characterized by hard internal body parts that did not exist in Cambrian chordates. Plenty of invertebrate animals make use of calcium carbonate to form shells and other supportive or protective structures and equipment for feeding, and some cephalopod molluscs, such as cuttlefish, have a simple internal "bone" that is used primarily as a buoyancy aid. However, only vertebrates have an internal skeleton of articulating bones, and bony jaws bearing rows of hard teeth to deal with their food.

Not all animals (prehistoric and modern) that are classed as vertebrates have all of these features, though. The precursor to bone (both in evolution and in individual development) is cartilage, and early in vertebrate ancestry there were animals with cartilage-based skulls and vertebral columns. The earliest vertebrates arose during the Cambrian explosion, and some were contemporaries of *Pikaia*, a chordate we have met already, which did not have vertebrate features at all. The species *Yunnanozoon lividum*, known from the important Maotianshan Shales in Yunnan, China, was a *Pikaia*-like organism that lived some 518 MYA. A detailed analysis of its fossils has revealed that its pharyngeal arches (structures in the head and jaw) contained cellular cartilage, a feature present only in vertebrates. The similar species *Myllokunmingia fengjiaoa*, known from the same fossil beds, had a cartilaginous cranium, as did its contemporary, *Haikouichthys*. The group Conodonta, predatory eel-like chordates that lived up to 520 million years ago, had eye anatomy typical of vertebrates, and also had pointed tooth-like structures in their jawless mouths.

The first vertebrates with true, bony jaws were very much what we would recognize as fishes, and lived about 445 MYA. They quickly replaced most of the jawless chordates living at the time and diversified greatly. One lineage, Sarcopterygii (the lobe-finned fishes) would go on to give rise to the first tetrapods and land-living vertebrates.

LOSE FORM, GAIN FUNCTION

Most of the four-limbed vertebrates, or tetrapods, have rather similar general body plans, whether they are frogs or foxes, crocodiles or cockatoos. However, their skeletal anatomy does show lots of variation—not just in the shape and size of their bones and teeth, but in the actual number they possess of each. All modern birds, of course, have no teeth at all, but they also have fewer and generally smaller bones than other tetrapods (some of these "missing" bones are absent entirely, and some are fused to other bones, making for a flight-friendly lightweight skeleton). Snakes and some lizards have lost their limbs entirely, while whales have lost their hind limbs, and many other mammals have lost part or all of their tails or teeth. Adaptation through evolution is as much about taking parts away as it is about adding and remodeling them—as flight became more important to early birds, and fast swimming became more important to early whales, so natural selection reshaped them into more efficient forms for these activities.

Above *A conodont, sporting the keen eyes and sharp teeth of a consummate hunter.*

Above *Hagfish, which first appeared in the Carboniferous, are unique among modern chordates in having a skull but no vertebral column.*

// Reaching for the skies—large land plants

If you have a variety of houseplants, you'll know well that some of them grow upwards, strongly, without assistance, while others tend to creep or to dangle over the edges of their pots. Modern Earth provides conditions suitable for all kinds of plant growth forms, but the ability to grow taller than your surroundings (including other plants), and to self-support so that you are not knocked down by the first gust of wind or passing arthropod, carries obvious advantages if your main goal in life is to absorb sunlight.

To achieve height, a land plant must have rigidity and a system for transporting nutrients to its far-flung parts. It must also have evolved some way to cope with the risk of desiccation, because even if it grows close to or even in water, its higher parts are likely to be permanently dry. Many mosses and liverworts lose water quite easily but can withstand becoming temporarily desiccated. A more versatile solution, though, is to avoid losing water in the first place. Fossilized plant spore cells from 455 MYA show signs of a

rigid and water-resistant cell wall, which is not present in algal spores.

Another step forward in controlling water balance came with the advent of vascular tissue. This is the plant's version of the circulatory system of animals—a network of vessels to carry water around inside the organism, and within that water a range of nutrients, waste products, hormones, and other biological compounds. The first evidence of vascular tissue in plants comes from the beginning of the Devonian Period and just before, with many species found in the Posongchong Formation in Yunnan, China. The most primitive vascular plants living today are the ferns, horsetails, club mosses, spike mosses and quillworts, all of which are spore-producing (not forming seeds or flowers). Some modern ferns and horsetails are relatively large, supported by their vascular

Above *Having vascular tissue enables ferns to grow much larger than non-vascular plants such as mosses.*

Left *Before true trees evolved, certain groups of simple plants, such as these* Lepidodendron, *developed tree-like proportions.*

systems, and while they tend to favor damp areas, they can also be found on drier terrain.

The biggest modern tree ferns, though, would be dwarfed by their relatives that lived on our planet millions of years ago. As well as giant tree ferns, the large early vascular plants included *Lepidodendron*, a genus related to the quillworts. Modern quillworts are small water-dwelling plants, whose leaves emerge from the water as a pincushion-like mass— these simple spear-shaped leaves are rarely more than 8 in (26.2 ft) long. However, some *Lepidodendron* specimens stood 98 ft (30 m) tall or more, and resembled true trees in form, with a sturdy main trunk from which leaves grew, but that eventually developed a branched crown. Extremely tall, tree-like horsetails also existed in these early forests, for example the 131 ft (40 m)-tall *Calamites*. All of these plants were abundant in the Carboniferous Period, but the advent of the first true trees led to their demise, and their surviving relatives are all far smaller.

// The first forests

With small plants spreading up and away from water, the land surface of our planet now offered more and better opportunities for animals to colonize, too. With the advent of tall plants such as *Lepidodendron*, rising high above the earlier plant life, the habitable land area for animals dramatically increased in three-dimensional space. Forests became widespread on Earth, and they characterized the Carboniferous Period of our world's history. Their legacy is the vast extent of coal beds that formed from their remains—a vital source of fossil fuel for us humans over the last few hundred years.

The first seed-bearing plants appeared in the late Devonian Period, evolving from a lineage of fern-like plants that had already developed strong, wood-like vascular tissue. These early seed-bearers had frond-like foliage, and their seeds developed inside cones or similar structures. These plants and their descendants (many of which are living today) are known as gymnosperms, meaning "naked seeds" because their seeds, though somewhat protected from the elements and seed-eating animals, are never fully enclosed in a pod or similar structure. Their open situation allows them to be fertilized by wind-borne pollen.

Carboniferous forests were soon dominated by tall gymnosperms, among them the cycads. There are a few species of cycads still living today, helping us to envisage what those ancient forests may have been like. These distinctive plants resemble palm trees and tree ferns, with a hefty trunk topped by a rosette-shaped crown of large leaves that have rows of long, fine leaflets on either side of a stout central stem. They have large elongated cones that sprout from the top of the trunk, among the bases of the leaves. The first true conifers emerged later in the Carboniferous Period, among them the cypress-like *Walchia*, whose fossilized stumps can still be seen today on the coast at the Brule fossil forest, Nova Scotia. The taxonomic order Voltziales, to which *Walchia* belonged, gave rise to numerous families, some of which in turn led to modern conifer lineages. Conifers in general thrived on Carboniferous Earth, and still dominate many areas of forested land on Earth today.

Below *The heyday of cycads was the mid-Paleozoic, but a few descendants of the lineage have survived to the modern day.*

SEEDS VS SPORES

The evolution of the seed is considered a landmark stage in the history of plant life. Spores, in plants, are simple female reproductive structures (often a single cell) that are usually fertilized by male reproductive cells after they have been shed from the parent plant and are in a place suitable for them to grow. In the case of seeds, the female reproductive cell or ovum is fertilized while still on the plant, by male reproductive cells in the form of pollen. By the time the ovum falls or is expelled from the parent plant, it has become a seed, with a durable outer coating. Inside, an embryo has developed, and a generous supply of protein- and fat-rich food has accumulated that will sustain the embryo through its early development. The fallen seed can lie dormant for some time, until conditions become suitable for germination. Seeds are more robust than spores, and are more likely to survive and successfully germinate, meaning that the parent plant tends to produce fewer of them. Seed-bearing plants rapidly out-competed spore-bearing plants in many land environments, and they are by far the more dominant of the two on modern Earth.

Above *Gymnosperm seeds develop in a woody cone, which offers protection (though not from specialized pine-seed eaters like this crossbill).*

Below *With a tough coat and a stock of food for the embryo inside, a seed has more chance of germinating successfully than a fragile spore.*

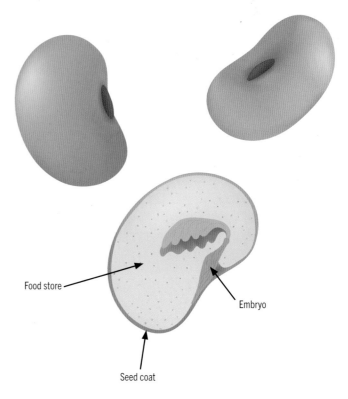

Food store

Embryo

Seed coat

// Giant invertebrates of the Carboniferous

Imagine you are walking through a Carboniferous rainforest. Underfoot, the terrain is spongy and swampy. All around you, the trunks of tree ferns and great cycads soar above, their broad frilled crowns shading you from the sunlight. The air feels incredibly rich and heavily scented. A sudden aerial rattle startles you—the sound of fast-beating wings. A bird? This is before the time of birds, however what dashes into the clearing above your head is certainly easily the size of many of the birds you know from your own time. But it is no bird—it's a colossal insect, a four-winged predator with huge eyes and strong legs ready to seize its prey. You are grateful that you are still considerably larger than this formidable hunter?

Those great forests of the middle to late Carboniferous are famed for the diversity of land arthropods they supported, but, even more than that, for the extraordinary size that some of those invertebrates attained. The dragonfly-like predators, known as griffinflies, had wingspans of up to 30 in (75 cm)—more recently evolved flying insects have never come close to their size. Yet even they seem diminutive compared to *Arthropleura*, a (thankfully) herbivorous millipede that grew to up to 8.5 ft (2.6 m) long. Add to the mix some colossal cockroaches, super-sized stoneflies, vast velvet worms, and scorpions not far shy of 3.3 ft (1 m) long, and you can imagine that, while these ancient landscapes lacked dinosaurs and more familiar prehistoric giants, they were certainly full of impressive and imposing animal life.

There were relatively few land-dwelling animals in the early Carboniferous. This is thought to be down to a temporary low in atmospheric oxygen, but the rise of land plants reversed the situation. Their photosynthesizing activities meant that atmospheric carbon dioxide was greatly reduced and oxygen greatly increased. This led in time to a change in climate, from the warm and humid conditions of the early Carboniferous to a much colder period later, which reduced rainforest cover over many parts of the land and consequently caused an extinction event among Carboniferous animals.

Above *Fossil* Meganeura, *a dragonfly-like insect with a 68 cm (26.7 in) wingspan.*

Below *Pre-dating the evolution of birds, the griffinflies were fearsome aerial predators of Carboniferous forests.*

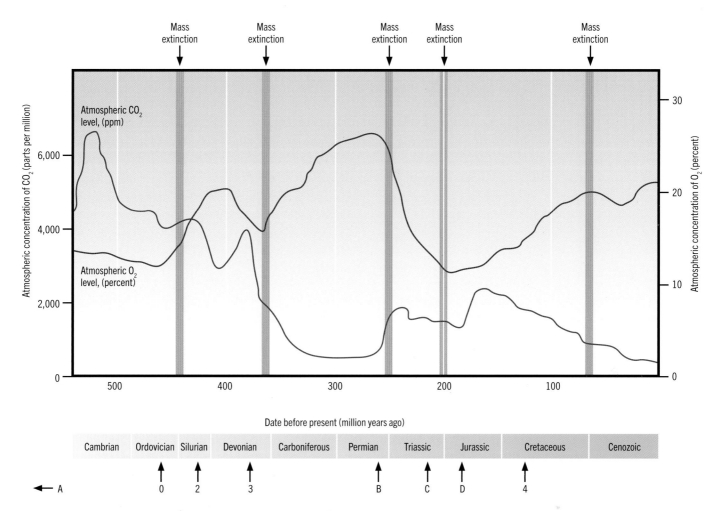

Mass extinction   Mass extinction   Mass extinction   Mass extinction   Mass extinction

Atmospheric CO_2 level, (ppm)

Atmospheric O_2 level, (percent)

Atmospheric concentration of CO_2 (parts per million)

Atmospheric concentration of O_2 (percent)

6,000

4,000

2,000

0

30

20

10

0

500   400   300   200   100

Date before present (million years ago)

| Cambrian | Ordovician | Silurian | Devonian | Carboniferous | Permian | Triassic | Jurassic | Cretaceous | Cenozoic |

← A   0   2   3   B   C   D   4

THE OXYGEN EQUATION

Why were insects and other arthropods so enormous in those forests, 300 million years ago, when today our land invertebrate animals are so small? The answer probably lies in the concentration of atmospheric oxygen. Oxygen levels peaked at more than 30 percent—today, oxygen makes up just 21 percent of our planet's atmospheric cocktail of gases. The respiratory system of arthropods is mainly passive, with oxygen entering their bodies via pores and then diffusing through a system of tubes (tracheae). Higher oxygen concentrations meant that more oxygen got in, allowing for greater growth. However, oxygen at high concentrations is also damaging and toxic to life, and it is likely that smaller arthropods were much more vulnerable to this than their larger cousins. Therefore, atmospheric conditions not only permitted greater size, but selected against smaller size, and it was only when the atmospheric conditions changed that smaller-bodied arthropods out-competed their giant cousins.

// Emergence (literally) of land vertebrates

Through the Devonian Period, ocean and freshwater fishes showed dramatic adaptive radiation, becoming highly diverse and abundant. For this reason, the Devonian is sometimes called "The age of fishes." Some of these early forms were quite remarkable in appearance, such as the armored, horn-nosed, and jawless *Pteraspis*, the huge *Dunkleosteus*, which had long blades instead of teeth and was the largest predator on Earth at the time, and *Brindabellaspis,* which had a snout like a platypus and a mud-rummaging foraging strategy to match. Fish with bony skeletons and toothy jaws were soon the dominant groups. The taxonomic class Chondrichthyes (rays and sharks) also thrived in the Devonian—these fishes have a mainly cartilaginous skeleton, but they evolved from bony ancestors.

The two main lineages of bony fishes living today are the ray-finned (Actinopterygii) and the lobe-finned (Sarcopterygii). The former group is by far the most successful, comprising some 99 percent of all modern bony fish species, and in both of these lineages some groups have adapted to be capable of breathing air. The most famous of the tiny number of lobe-finned fishes around now are the coelacanths, known only from Cretaceous fossils until a living specimen was caught in 1938; a second extant species was found in 1999. We nickname these fish "living fossils" as, to our eyes, they have changed little over many millions of years. However, not all lobe-finned fish lineages fit this mold—this was the group that gave rise to the first tetrapods, and in turn the first walking, land-dwelling vertebrates.

The pectoral and pelvic fins of lobe-finned fishes are noticeably fleshy with a distinct "stem," and have a different bony anatomy to those of ray-finned fishes. In particular, they are supported by a single sturdy bone, which is analogous to the humerus and femur in tetrapod forelimbs and hind limbs respectively. Many early lobe-finned fishes would have used their strong fins to rest and also move on the seabed and, like modern lungfishes (which, besides the coelacanths, are the only other group of lobe-finned fishes alive today), some developed air-breathing lungs that worked alongside their gills. The lungs developed from the swim bladders that most fish possess, and which primarily function as a way to control buoyancy. A range of fossil animals with intermediate characteristics between lobe-finned fishes and four-legged amphibians have been discovered through the early 21st century, illustrating how the ability to breathe and move on land progressed over time.

FINDING *TIKTAALIK*

The first fossils of the fish *Tiktaalik* were found in 2004. The oldest specimen was 383 MYA. *Tiktaalik* shows several traits typical of tetrapods, including the anatomy of its rib bones, and a distinct mobile neck that was separate from its pectoral girdle. This animal is notable in that its existence and likely age were predicted in some detail by palaeontologists before it was actually discovered—everything we knew of evolutionary history at the time indicated that animals like this would have lived at that time. Subsequently, true four-limbed tetrapod fossils have been found, such as *Acanthostega*, which lived some 365 MYA and resembled a large salamander, though it was likely to be entirely aquatic—its anatomy would not have supported it enough to walk on land. A candidate for the first that could do this is the more robust (and even bigger) *Ichthyostega*, a 4.9 ft (1.5 m) seven-toed tetrapod that was probably able to move like a seal on shorelines.

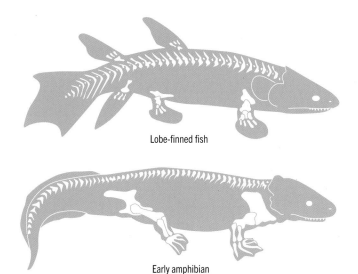

Lobe-finned fish

Early amphibian

Left *Fossilized tracks of* Ichthyostega, *an early land-walking relative of modern tetrapods.*

Below *Although mudskippers can breathe air and walk (after a fashion) on land, they belong to the ray-finned fish lineage and are not related to modern tetrapods.*

// Free from the water—the essential amniote egg

If you have ever seen frogspawn, you'll have noticed how soft and jelly-like it is in texture, and how all the individual eggs are stuck together to form a cloud-like mass. It's obvious that this clump of potential frogs needs to stay in water and that prolonged exposure to the air would not do it any good at all. The new-born tadpoles are fish-like rather than frog-like in form, adapted to immediately settle into the watery environment in which they find themselves.

Not all amphibians—indeed not all frogs—place their spawn directly into a body of water, but amphibian eggs, like fish eggs, do all need wetness around them at this stage in their lives. These eggs, with their covering of soft jelly that is permeable to water, are like the prehistoric, aquatic precursors of land plants, land arthropods, and land vertebrates—they have no resistance to desiccation and their structural integrity relies on the support of the water around them. Therefore, amphibians need access to sufficient water, even if they don't need to live in it for their whole life cycle. Forming an egg that could survive prolonged exposure to the air was one of the key adaptations that enabled vertebrate animals to continue to spread and thrive across the land.

Amphibian egg

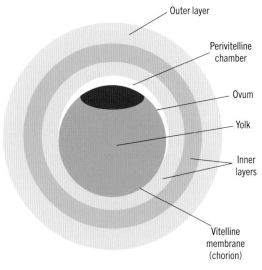

- Outer layer
- Perivitelline chamber
- Ovum
- Yolk
- Inner layers
- Vitelline membrane (chorion)

Reptile egg

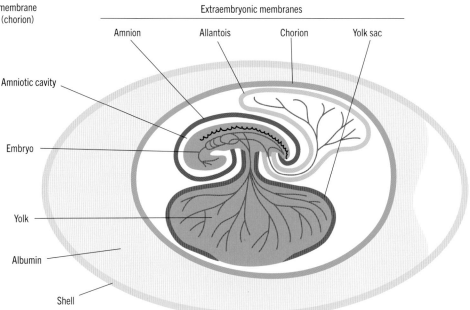

Extraembryonic membranes

- Amnion
- Allantois
- Chorion
- Yolk sac
- Amniotic cavity
- Embryo
- Yolk
- Albumin
- Shell

Above *Comparison between the structure of an amphibian egg and a reptile egg.*

The amniote egg is more complex in structure than the anamniotic eggs of amphibians, with several membranes and an outer shell. This shell is porous but the inner membranes regulate what can pass through it. The first amniotes evolved about 312 MYA, from newt- or salamander-like amphibian ancestors. Neither their eggs nor their newly hatched young needed to be in water to survive. Their other adaptations for a more land-based existence included a tougher, more waterproof skin, and more efficient breathing mechanisms. Gills were lost, and so (mostly) was the ability to carry out gas exchange through the skin—this "skin breathing" remains an important additional ability in some amphibians and fish. Amniotes had a freedom to live on dry land that only the arthropods had enjoyed before them, and the way that they breathed meant that their evolutionary pathways had very different limitations than those that affected arthropod evolution. Consequently, they were to evolve relatively rapidly into an array of forms with tremendous diversity in size, shape, and way of life.

TWO PATHS

The modern amniotes fall into three familiar groupings—reptiles, birds, and mammals. These categories make sense to us, as the differences between the groups are so clear-cut and obvious. However, the true picture is that there are two foundational lineages of amniotes—the synapsids and the sauropsids, which diverged from one another very soon after the first amniotes appeared. The key difference between them, initially, lay in their skull anatomy, with synapsids developing an additional opening (fenestra) in the skull behind the eye socket. This small difference was the start of dramatic divergence, with modern mammals eventually evolving from these early synapsids. Further along in evolutionary history, one lineage of sauropsids developed two such openings in their skulls—this lineage, Diapsida, gave rise to all modern reptiles. The dinosaurs are also diapsids, and modern birds evolved from a dinosaur lineage. All other forms of sauropsids (known collectively as anapsids) that evolved no additional fenestrae are long extinct. The turtles and tortoises were once thought to be anapsids, as their skulls lack additional openings, but studies now indicate that they are indeed diapsids that have lost their extra fenestrae.

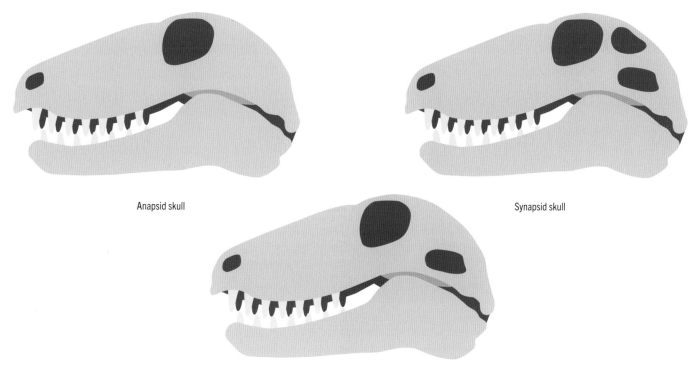

Anapsid skull

Synapsid skull

Diapsid skull

Above *Diagram of anapsid, synapsid and diapsid skulls.*

// Paleozoic ice ages

Our planet's climate is governed by a complex interplay of factors. We sit in the right position within the Solar System to be warmed but not roasted by our Sun, and life on Earth has enjoyed more than 4 billion years of existence despite something of a climate roller coaster. However, when global temperatures have dipped to extreme lows, causing an ice age, the impact on life of all kinds has been dramatic, wiping out vast numbers of individual organisms and a great many species of all kinds. In the wake of an ice age, though, the scene is set for another explosion of adaptive radiation as the survivors make the most of an array of new opportunities to establish new ecological niches and, in due course, entire new ecosystems.

The first ice age of the Paleozoic took place toward the end of the Ordovician Period, around 440–460 MYA. At this time, most of the Earth's land masses were in the southern hemisphere, and these land areas became extensively glaciated. Evidence for this short but very sharp period of extreme cold comes from rock deposits associated with glaciation in modern north Africa and Arabia, as well as the presence in rock of that age of certain isotopes of carbon and oxygen that are associated with dramatic cooling. This evidence suggests that tropical sea temperatures dropped by 18°F (10°C), and sea levels also fell sharply. These factors combined to cause the extinction of more than 60 percent

of all marine life, although relatively few entire lineages were wiped out. The cause of the shift in climate is not known for certain, although a significant meteor strike about 470 MYA could have triggered it, by creating a denser, dustier atmosphere that reflected the Sun's heat.

Following this ice age and the resultant Ordovician-Silurian mass extinction, temperatures rose again into the Devonian Period. Later into the Carboniferous Period, the proliferation of land plants caused a fall in atmospheric carbon dioxide levels, setting a string of ice ages into motion through the end of the Carboniferous Period and the beginning of the Permian Period. The climate was further destabilized by tectonic movement, with land masses beginning to collide together to form the supercontinent Pangaea. This huge land mass, surrounded by the vast deep ocean Panthalassa, experienced climate variation much more extreme than that of a world composed of smaller land masses separated by shallower stretches of sea. It was a fall in plant abundance and the associated rise in atmospheric carbon dioxide (as there were fewer photosynthesizing plants around to consume it) that brought about the end of the "Late Paleozoic Ice House."

Below *This timeline shows the interplay between atmospheric carbon dioxide, and the occurrence of ice ages.*

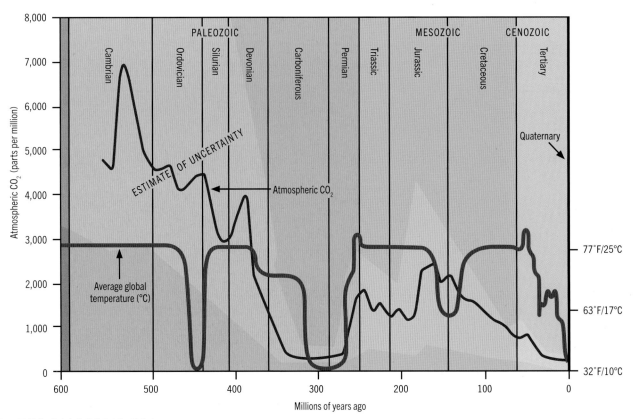

CLIMATE THEN AND NOW

Those who deny the existence and/or impact of human-caused (anthropogenic) climate change, here in the 21st century, often point to the Earth's early history and the great fluctuations in global temperature that our planet has survived up until now. Climate change is indeed natural, and arguably the climate change we are experiencing today is no less natural—we humans are as much a product of evolution as any other animal, after all. However, the pace of anthropogenic climate change is beyond anything history has to show us. And we must remember that climate change in prehistory caused countless extinctions, just as it is doing today.

Below *A "snowball Earth." Our planet's history is punctuated by regular ice ages, and associated impacts on living things.*

// Pangaea

The patterns of tectonic movement and the consequent non-stop movement of Earth's land masses mean that every once in a while, as we progress through the millennia, a supercontinent is formed. By definition, this is a continent formed from most or all of the land on the planet, and as the Paleozoic Era neared its end, the most famous of all supercontinents ever to exist was slowly forming.

Pangaea may be the best known of historical supercontinents, but it was far from the first. Depending on criteria, up to ten have existed before. One of these was Gondwana, which formed early in the Paleozoic from the consolidation of what are now South America, Africa, Arabia, Madagascar, India, Australia, and Antarctica. Gondwana was centered over the South Pole and covered about a fifth of the Earth's surface. The other major land area at that time was Laurasia, formed from what is now North America and much of Europe. Laurasia first made contact with Gondwana in the late Devonian Period, and Pangaea began to form.

Since Pangaea's break-up, the continental masses have moved apart, and our map of modern Earth is very different.

However, the old connections are still apparent, most strikingly in how the east coast of South America fits like a super-sized jigsaw piece against the west coast of Africa, and also in the patterns of fossil distribution of land animals and plants that were living at the time, showing that their intercontinental ranges were once connected.

The meeting of two great land masses through tectonic plate movement is not a rushed affair, nor is it a peaceful one. Mountain ranges are formed where land masses meet—in this case, when Laurasia and Gondwana collided, the Central Pangaean Mountains came into being, and by mid-Permian times they were comparable in height and extent to today's Himalayas. They formed a considerable geographic barrier to animal movement and had dramatic effects upon the climate, seasons, and weather. Pangaea's formation also meant the creation of a continuous deep global ocean, a great reduction in the extent of shallow coastal seas, and vast tracts of land that were thousands of miles away from coasts and other water sources.

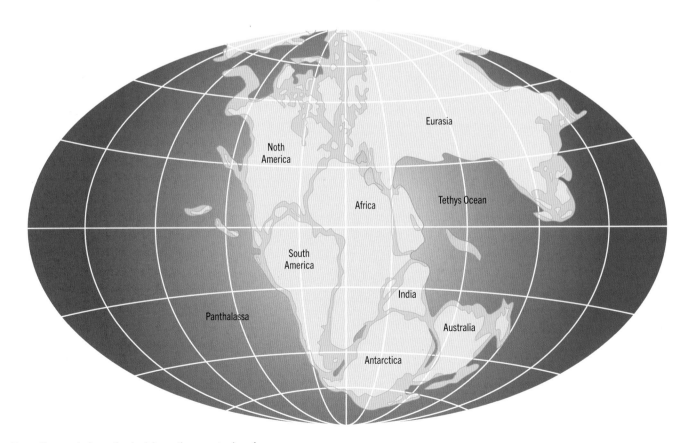

Above *Pangaea's formation had dramatic repercussions for Earth's climate and distribution of habitats.*

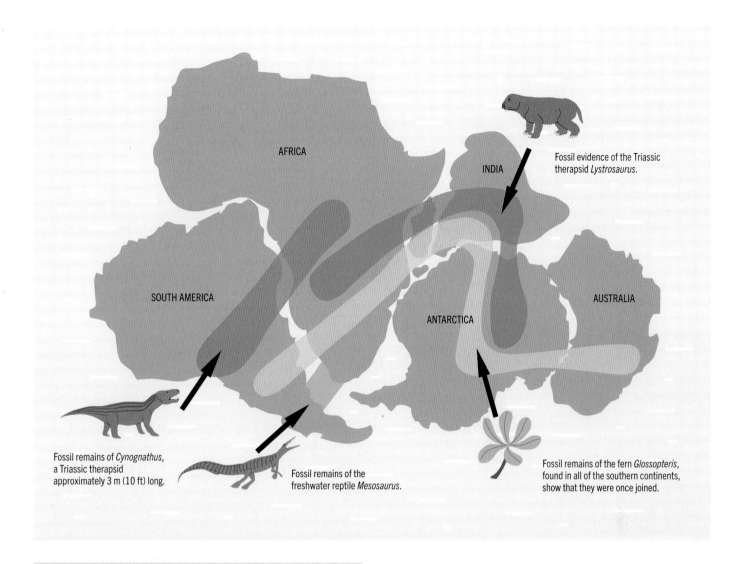

AFRICA

INDIA

Fossil evidence of the Triassic therapsid *Lystrosaurus*.

SOUTH AMERICA

ANTARCTICA

AUSTRALIA

Fossil remains of *Cynognathus*, a Triassic therapsid approximately 3 m (10 ft) long.

Fossil remains of the freshwater reptile *Mesosaurus*.

Fossil remains of the fern *Glossopteris*, found in all of the southern continents, show that they were once joined.

THE NEXT SUPERCONTINENT

We can predict the future movement of tectonic plates to some extent, based on past and present observations. One of these predictions is that, somewhere between 50 million and 200 million years from now, a new supercontinent (named Amasia) will form, as the Pacific narrows and eventually closes, bringing North America into contact with Asia. Amasia is predicted to be centered on the North Pole, and to be less compact in form than Pangaea—it may also not include the land masses that are currently Australia and Antarctica. What is certain is that, if Amasia forms, it will have a far-reaching range of effects on whatever life is present on Earth at that point.

Above *The distribution of certain fossils reveals previous continental positions in Earth's history.*

The Permian mass extinction

Death is a fact of life, and so too is extinction—the death of an entire species (or genus, or worse). Extinctions have been occurring ever since life first appeared on our world. Evolution by natural selection refines each new generation of an organism to be better adapted to survive and prosper in its environment, and it also allows the population to gradually adapt to change. However, adverse changes often occur too quickly for natural selection to keep up, and this is when declines and extinctions occur.

Throughout the history of life, we see a 'background extinction rate' of species, but this is punctuated by a few dramatic spikes, when extinction rates increased very sharply over a relatively short period of time. The biggest of all occurred at the end of the Permian Period, about 251 MYA. This catastrophe, the Permian-Triassic extinction event, consisted of three distinct close-together waves, the last being the most severe, which between them brought about

the demise of about 90 percent of all species and 57 percent of all families living on Planet Earth at the time. Devastation of this scale is hard to imagine, especially when we know that an equally dramatic recovery took place to restore diverse and abundant life across our planet once again.

The formation of Pangaea is one likely cause of the extinction of marine life in particular. Coastlines and shallow seas support far more life than deep ocean, and the loss of this habitat as the supercontinent formed was very extensive. On the land itself, there would have been extensive inland areas where little rain fell, and these habitats would have been fairly inhospitable to life. However, of greater consequence was a prolonged spell of violent volcanic eruptions, particularly in the area known today as the Siberian Traps (now located in Siberia). Tectonic plate movement is often associated with increased volcanic activity, and in this case the eruptions produced vast

Below *Fossil brachiopods from the Permian. These animals resemble bivalve molluscs.*

Above *The synapsid* Dimetrodon *lived (and died) during the Permian. Its distinctive "sail" back probably helped with temperature regulation.*

amounts of ash clouds, released great quantities of hydrogen sulphite, methane and carbon dioxide, and ignited coal beds, causing fires. This would have poisoned and deoxygenated the sea water, and caused acid rain and a dramatic greenhouse effect that rapidly elevated atmospheric temperatures. Conditions on Earth became highly hostile to many forms of life, in a way not seen perhaps since the Hadean Eon.

The many casualties included the trilobites, which had been so successful through the Paleozoic Era, along with all tabulate and rugose corals. Among molluscs, many groups, including a large number of gastropods and cephalopods,

were lost and the mollusc-like brachiopods were also dramatically affected. On land, two-thirds of amphibians and reptiles disappeared, along with one-third of insects. The synapsids, including the lineage known as therapsids, which were ancestral to modern mammals, were also very severely affected. The picture is less clear for land plants—many may have survived the worst of the hostile conditions thanks to their resilient seeds. It's also significant that, at this time in biological history, the interdependencies we see today between plants and animals (the latter acting as pollinators and seed dispersers) had not yet been established.

// A handful of survivors—the founders of Mesozoic life

The volcanoes that formed the rocky ranges of the Siberian Traps were violently and destructively active for about 2 million years. This could be described as a brief interlude in geological time. However, for us, with our individual lifespans of a few decades and our collective lifespan (so far) as a species of well under half a million years, it is a timescale that's difficult to comprehend. As for Pangaea, a land configuration so much less hospitable to life than a more dispersed arrangement of land masses, it existed for at least 73 million years. The pressure of natural selection on Earth's plants and animals was at an all-time high, and only the toughest and luckiest survived. We must also remember that, even among the survivors, losses of individuals would often have been very high and some of the species that got through would have done so by the slimmest of margins.

Among land vertebrates and some other groups, body size was a significant predictor of survival chances. Smaller animals generally did better than large ones—their energetic needs were lower, which was an advantage as food of all kinds became scarcer. Smaller animals also tend to have a more rapid life cycle and higher reproductive rate, meaning that they could bounce back from severe population reductions. It was also greatly beneficial to have a generalized diet and adaptable habitat needs, meaning an ability to move between ecological niches, although some extreme specialists (such as deep-sea species) did survive due to their particular habitat being naturally protected from the hazards.

One example of a true survivor was *Lystrosaurus*, which existed in the form of about six species in the Permian Period. If we saw one of these pig-sized animals today, we would probably decide it was a peculiar lizard, with its sprawling gait and beaked face. However, it was actually a therapsid, a member of the group of synapsids from which mammals eventually evolved. It was a stout and stocky animal with

Above *The synapsid genus* Lystrosaurus *was highly successful in the aftermath of the Permian mass extinction.*

Above Arizonasaurus, *a Triassic dinosaur that evolved a similar body shape to late Permian synapsids like* Dimetrodon.

thick, solid limbs and a large, reinforced head that probably helped it to burrow and earned it the nickname "shovel lizard." *Lystrosaurus* scraped through the Permian-Triassic mass extinction, perhaps in the form of just a single, small species (although it was still very much at the larger end of the vertebrate survivors). Its survival may be attributed to its burrowing ability, and the growth patterns of its fossils suggest it may have been able to enter a hibernation-like state for prolonged periods. It also appeared to have a generalized lifestyle, providing adaptability that insulated it from the hostile environment. The surviving *Lystrosaurus* species thrived as conditions eased into the early Triassic, and they radiated into a large variety of new species, soon becoming by far the most abundant land vertebrates over a broad swathe of southern Pangaea.

PAVING THE WAY

In the wake of a mass extinction, there are great opportunities. For the animals that made it into the Mesozoic Era, the survival of many Paleozoic plants meant that a relatively quick bounce-back in population and diversity was almost inevitable. Some lineages were lost forever, but this made way for new forms to adapt and diversify. Among them were the archosaurs, a lineage of diapsids that thrived in the late Paleozoic but were greatly reduced by the dawn of the Mesozoic. Archosaurs and therapsids were competitors in many respects, but the open-opportunities world of the early Triassic allowed both forms to thrive, and as the Mesozoic progressed, the archosaurs became the dominant land vertebrates—a role they held for many millions of years.

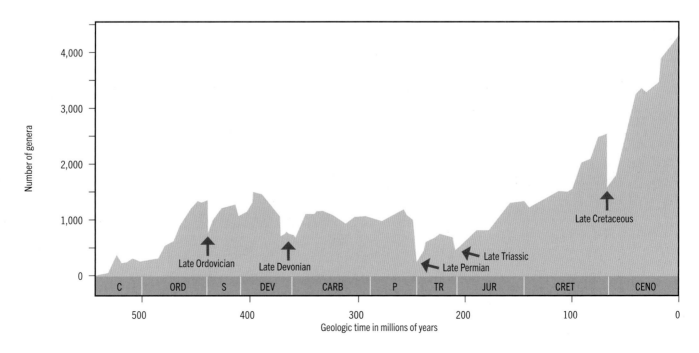

THE MESOZOIC ERA

In the aftermath of the Permian mass extinction, a drastically thinned-out population of survivors inherited an Earth full of ecological opportunity. Improving environmental conditions sparked the radiation of a host of new forms of life, adapting and evolving across land and sea. Most notable among these were the dinosaurs, which dominated terrestrial habitats, while huge marine reptiles hunted an increasingly diverse array of fishes and cephalopods, and pterosaurs took to the air. Climatic changes benefited some of these lineages and wiped out others, but it was the aftermath of a huge meteor strike that finally ended this era of giants.

Mamenchisaurus were a genus of sauropod dinosaur known for their strikingly long necks which made up nearly half the total body length.

// Overview of the era

With the end of the Permian Period and its devastating mass extinction that consigned so many species permanently to history, the Paleozoic Era came to an end and the Mesozoic Era began. This era spanned 252 to 65 MYA, and we divide it into three periods—the Triassic, Jurassic and Cretaceous. These three names are rather more familiar to most of us than the periods that preceded them, because of their connection with the "age of the dinosaurs.' It serves us well to remember, though, that this era spanned nearly 200 million years, meaning that many dinosaurs lived much closer to our own time than they did to the days of the first Triassic dinosaurs.

Through the Triassic Period, Pangaea began to break up and the Earth's land masses were once again increasingly separated by considerable expanses of water. This affected the distribution of land animals and plants, meaning that some lineages were split in two (or more), and in their isolation they proceeded to evolve in different ways, as suited the particular conditions of the land on which they found themselves. Pangaea's break-up also recreated shallower inshore and coastal habitats, ideal for marine-dwelling Permian survivors to proliferate and evolve into more diverse and specialized forms.

Besides the dinosaurs, other large vertebrate animals evolved through this era, including the first flying vertebrates in the form of pterosaurs. This era also saw the rise of a range of large marine tetrapods that emerged from land-dwelling ancestors but became as well adapted to their environment as the fish that preceded them, and the whales and dolphins that were to follow in the future. The feather, one of nature's greatest masterpieces, evolved in the mid-Mesozoic, and was a feature of many subsequent dinosaur lineages. Feathers were originally a means of thermoregulation and probably a canvas for color, but by 160 or 150 MYA, they were to reach their most refined expression as tools for flight in winged dinosaurs—including birds.

The latter part of this era also saw the evolution of angiosperms—flowering plants. This group of plants quickly became very successful and diverse, and new, mutually beneficial relationships were forged between them and a huge range of animal species. To attract and make use of animal pollinators, flowers evolved elaborate shapes and colors, and sweet (though sometimes not so sweet) scents, and, once spent, some flowers developed into succulent fruits to attract seed-dispersers.

Age (Ma)

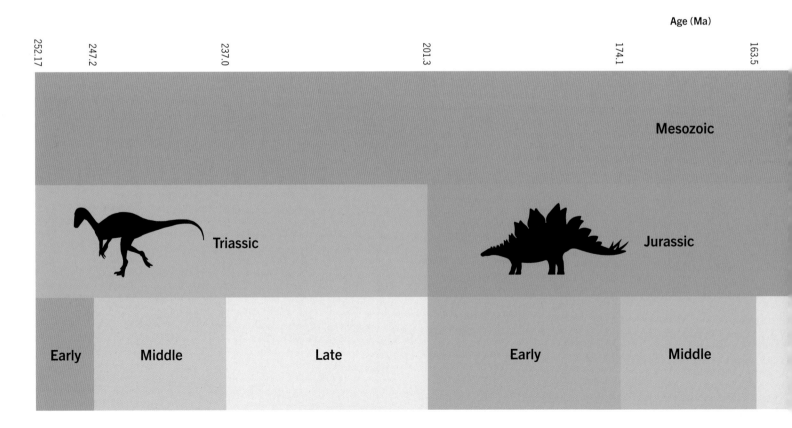

252.17   247.2   237.0   201.3   174.1   163.5

Mesozoic

Triassic   Jurassic

Early   Middle   Late   Early   Middle

Above *A* Tyrannosaurus *confronts a* Stegosaurus—*this scenario would never have occurred in reality, as the two species lived more than 70 million years apart.*

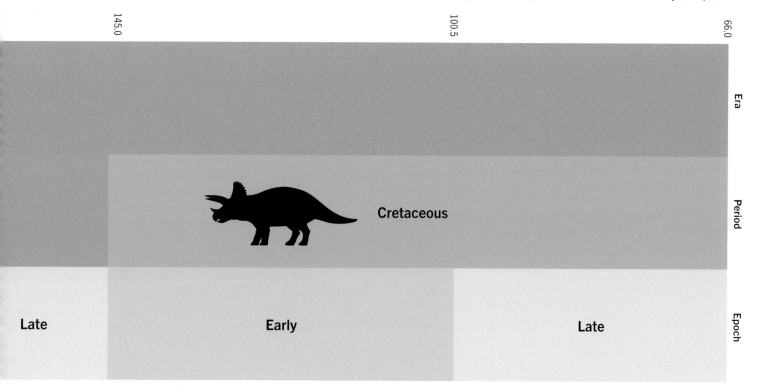

145.0

100.5

66.0

Era

Cretaceous

Period

Late

Early

Late

Epoch

// A radiation of ray-finned fish

Through the later Paleozoic Era, fish diversity increased greatly. The sharks and rays were especially species-rich, and included some peculiar forms such as *Stethacanthus*, which had a broad, flattened top to its dorsal fin, and *Belantsea*, which had a flattened and dramatically humped body and tightly spaced, forward-pointing triangular teeth that allowed its mouth to work as a rock-grazing beak. Many of these forms disappeared in the Permian-Triassic mass extinction, as did many lobe-finned fishes, and it was the turn of the bony, ray-finned fishes to become dominant. In particular, one sub-group, the teleosts (notable for their

extendable mouths), was especially successful, and today 96 percent of all living fish species are teleosts.

Some of the more notable genera to emerge through the Mesozoic included the Triassic *Saurichthys*, which were possibly among the first ray-finned fish whose eggs hatched internally, meaning that the female gave birth to live young. These were large and very slim, streamlined predators with long snouts, capable of great bursts of speed, which they used when ambush-hunting other fish. In the Jurassic Period, the order Pachycormiformes emerged, with their long, swordfish-like snouts and greatly elongated and

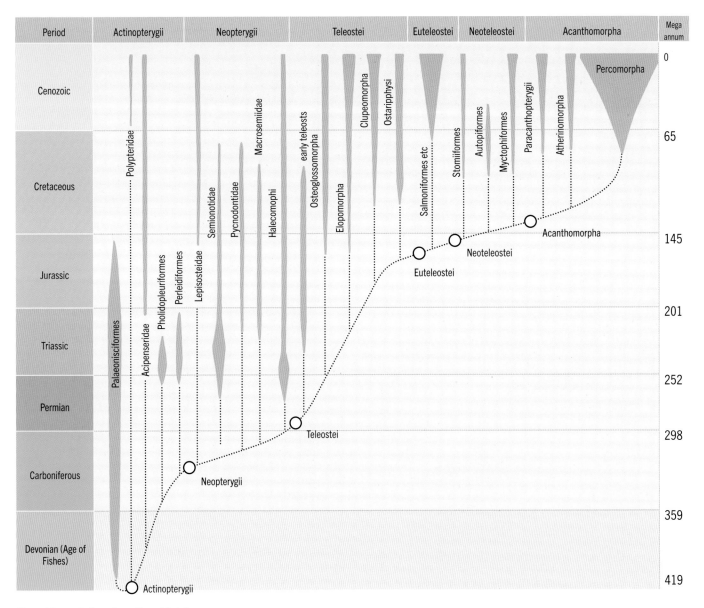

Above *The evolution of ray-finned fish lineages.*

serrated pectoral fins. This period also saw the appearance of *Leedsichthys*, a genus of robust, filter-feeding fish that included the largest teleost species ever to exist, with some specimens exceeding 65.6 ft (20 m) in length.

Several of the fish lineages that emerged in the Mesozoic are still around today and include some of the best-known and most successful groups, such as the order Clupeiformes (herrings and anchovies), which appeared in the mid-Jurassic, and the salmonids, which first appeared in the late Jurassic. The very large group Percomorpha, which includes modern cichlids, flatfish, gobies, seahorses, pufferfish, and many more, appeared in the late Cretaceous Period. Some more obscure extant lineages are also of Mesozoic origin, such as the peculiar bony-tongued fish (Osteoglossomorpha), first noted from the early Triassic.

PLANT-BASED DIET

In land-based ecosystems, we think of photosynthesizing plants as the foundational tier—the producers—and plant-eating animals as the next level up. The herbivores greatly outnumber the carnivores that feed on them (the other way around would be inherently unstable). However, the primary producers in the sea are cyanobacteria and other phytoplankton, which are in turn eaten by non-photosynthesizing zooplankton (including some tiny and larval animals but also non-animal microbes). The vast majority of marine animals of any appreciable size feed on other animals. Some fish today are herbivores, grazing on algae that grow on rocks, but herbivory in fish evolved relatively late in their history. One of the first to do so was *Hemicaplyterus*, which lived in the early Mesozoic. It was small with a deep, flattened body, like a modern angelfish, and each of its teeth had multiple points, adapted for algae-scraping.

Above *A fossil fish of the genus* Lycoptera, *part of the bony-tongued fish lineage that first appeared in the late Jurassic.*

Triassic triumphs—early archosaur groups

The diapsids were the only lineage of the early reptilian lineage Sauropsida to make it to modern times. Modern diapsids fall into two groups—the lepidosaurs (lizards and snakes) and the archosaurs (birds and crocodilians, and probably also turtles, although their correct taxonomic position is not universally agreed by palaeontologists). The archosaurs today exist alongside the mammals that emerged from the other fundamental reptilian lineage, Synapsida. Archosaurs probably first appeared just before the Permian-Triassic mass extinction. As the Triassic began and Earth's conditions became more hospitable to life, the surviving archosaurs and synapsids—along with other reptilian lineages that are no longer with us today—spread, diversified and soon came into competition with each other for ecological niches.

In the early Triassic, as we have seen, one particular genus of synapsids was overwhelmingly successful above all other large land vertebrates—*Lystrosaurus*. It occurred throughout Pangaea, and different populations persisted on different land masses as the supercontinent began to break up. However, as the Triassic progressed, the archosaurs began to take over, becoming more diverse and occupying more niches than *Lystrosaurus* or any other synapsids.

One of the key advancements that occurred early in Triassic archosaurs was the move to upright rather than sprawling limbs. The sprawling, wide-legged gait inherited from their amphibian ancestors meant that early land-dwelling archosaurs and synapsids alike were not very efficient walkers and runners, but as they became further separated from aquatic life, there was strong selective

Above *Two fossil archosaurs from the Triassic - a predatory rauisuchid on the left, and a herbivorous aetosaur on the right.*

pressure for change. The hip and shoulder anatomy of both lineages moved them toward a more upright gait, but the archosaurs' progress in this respect was more rapid. By the mid-Triassic, our planet once again had a thriving large-bodied, land-dwelling vertebrate fauna, but instead of the synapsids of the late Paleozoic, these were archosaurs, and among them were the first dinosaurs.

Archosauria's two main branches diverged from each other in the early Triassic. The group Pseudosuchia emerged in the early Triassic—this highly successful group was ancestral to modern crocodiles, and in its heyday included armored plant-eating forms such as the aetosaurs, and fast-running bipeds like the 220 lb (100 kg) *Poposaurus*, as well as more recognizably crocodile-like animals. The other branch of Archosauria is Avemetatarsalia. Triassic representatives of this group included the slender, lizard-like aphanosaurids, the small bipedal lagerpetids, the more heavy-set, long-legged quadrupedal herbivores that formed the family Silesauridae, and the first true pterosaurs and dinosaurs.

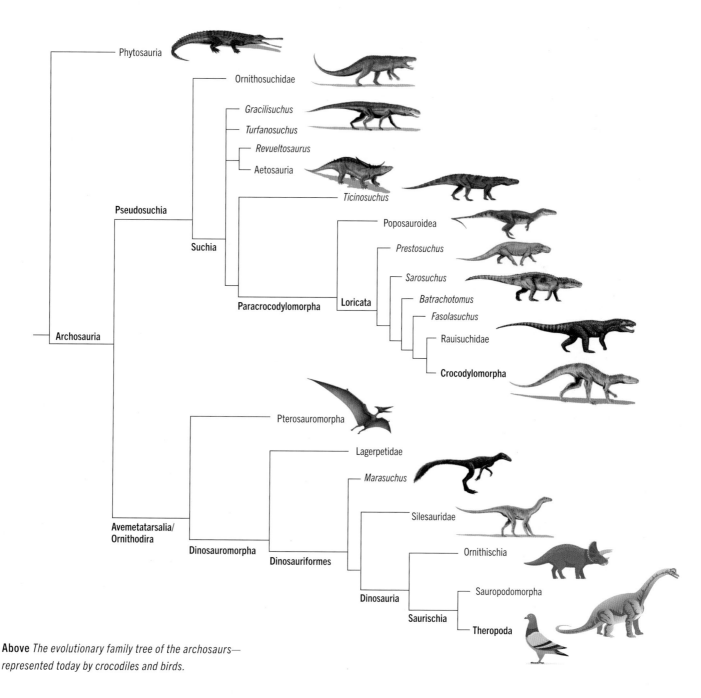

Above *The evolutionary family tree of the archosaurs—represented today by crocodiles and birds.*

// The slow return of continents

Pangaea remained in place through the Triassic Period. However, by 200 MYA, significant rifts had opened up on either side of the point where Laurasia and Gondwanaland had come together to form the supercontinent. Down in the south of Gondwanaland, the land masses of today's Australia and Antarctica were also beginning to move away from the main mass of Pangaea. The slow separation of the Earth's main land masses had, as we have seen, a wide range of consequences for life of all kinds.

We can see active rifts in various places on Earth today. They appear at the points where parts of the lithosphere (the Earth's rigid, rocky outer crust plus the part of the mobile upper mantle just below) are being pulled apart by tectonic movement. Rifts may be on land or below the sea—an example of the former is the Rift Valley in eastern Africa, where 4,350 miles (7,000 km) of lowlands and lakes marks the point where the African plate is being broken into two new, smaller tectonic plates. This rift is connected to the Red Sea rift, where separation between the African and Arabian plates is forming a widening trough in the form of the Red Sea.

The rift that formed in eastern Pangaea is known as the Tethys Sea, while in the west several rifts formed, one of which eventually became the north Atlantic. As gradual movement continued, Laurasia and Gondwanaland both separated into smaller land masses, and by the end of the Cretaceous Period, the configuration of the continents had taken on a shape that is quite familiar to our 21st-century eyes (though many more changes were still to come). However, these continents carry their history with them. The discovery and dating of fossils of animals, including *Lystrosaurus*, which once ranged across the vast continuous lands of Pangaea, reveal these ancient connections and separations that have shifted the land masses across our world over the last quarter of a billion years.

PLUMES AND TECTONIC MOVEMENT

We know that the seven major and numerous minor tectonic plates that make up the lithosphere are constantly in motion, and so our land masses will continue to change position gradually. This is believed to happen because of the heat and currents that affect the asthenosphere—the layer of mantle that lies below the lithosphere. Here, the rock is a hot and viscous liquid, and under the influence of convection currents, plumes of this material (known as magma) push up between the plates. Depending on which plates are affected, this can push land masses together or pull them apart. Geological activity of many kinds occurs between plate boundaries—rifts form when they separate, and mountains when they come together, while volcanic eruptions and earthquakes can be common along any plate boundaries.

Three types of plate boundary

Divergent plate boundary—plates that are moving apart

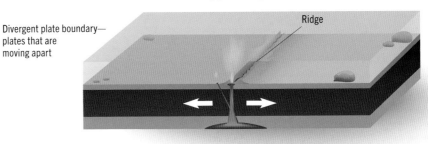

Ridge

Transform plate boundary—plates that are moving parallel to each other

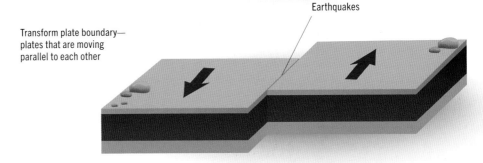

Earthquakes

Convergent plate boundary—plates that are moving together, with one sliding over the other

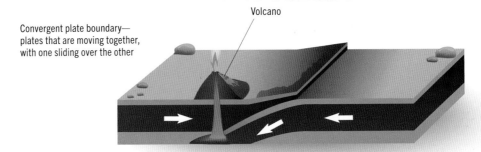

Volcano

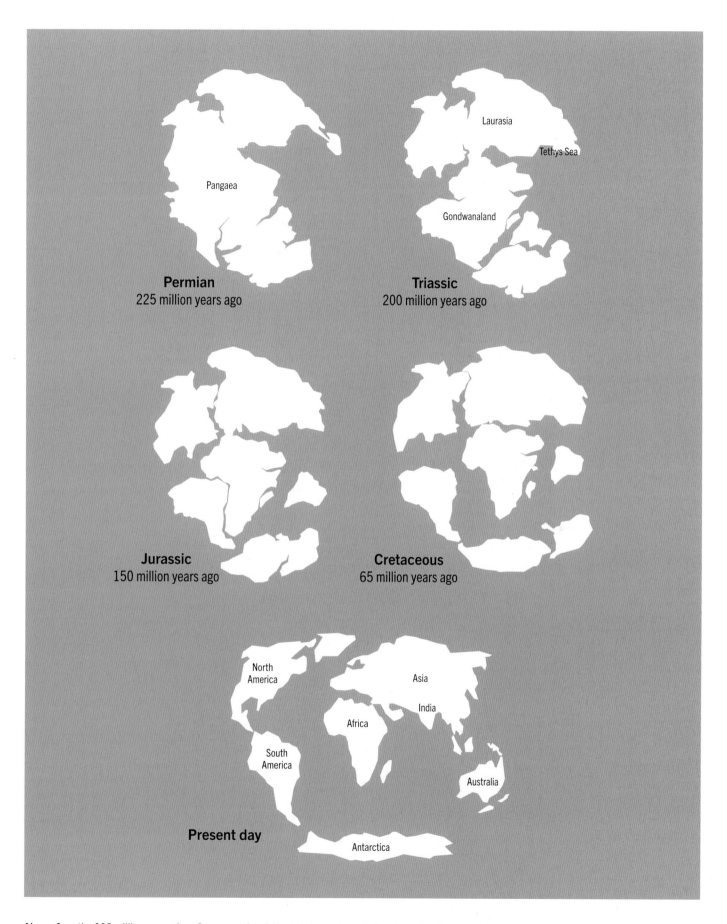

Above *Over the 225 million years since Pangaea existed, the continents have drifted toward their present-day positions.*

// Reefs and reptiles of the sea

In the Permian-Triassic mass extinction, two major groups of corals—tabulate and rugose—were wiped out. These marine animals belonged to the phylum Cnidaria (alongside jellyfish and sea anemones), and in their early lives were free-swimming and a component of zooplankton. As they matured, they settled on to the seabed, where they secreted cells of calcium carbonate to protect themselves. Some were solitary, but those that lived colonially formed coral reefs, which provided shelter for a large variety of other sea animals. Reefs can create lagoons of permanently warm, shallow water, and offer a solid foothold for algae and a range of sessile animals. They also provide refuge for juvenile fish from larger predators, which cannot pursue them through the stony mazes and into natural fissures and crevices.

Below *Sea snakes are among the modern reptile groups which bear live young rather than laying eggs.*

We know the two major groups of corals only from their diverse and beautiful fossils, which show that they were mostly found in equatorial regions and began to decline through the Permian Period, as the ocean became deeper and shallow shorelines became scarcer. However, other coral forms survived the extinction, or evolved not long after it, and they thrived in the early Mesozoic as sea conditions changed. In particular, the hard scleractinian corals became key reef-builders through the Triassic.

Alongside the animals that had an unbroken evolutionary history as marine-dwellers, the Triassic seas were also home to reptiles that had descended from terrestrial ancestors. The return to the sea did not mean a reversion of the evolutionary changes that had adapted these animals to the land in the first place. They did not regrow gills, exchange tough water-resistant skin for the soft, permeable skin of their amphibian ancestors, and nor did their eggs lose their additional membranes and shells. Nevertheless, reptiles from several different lineages adapted to life in the ocean, in different ways, during the early Mesozoic. They included the lizard-like thalattosaurs—slender, paddle-tailed fish-eaters, the very first ichthyosaurs (some of which were later to evolve an extremely fish-like shape), and early placodonts, broad-bodied and snub-nosed animals that resembled long-tailed, shell-less turtles.

VIVIPARITY

One of the biggest obstacles for a reptile returning to a marine life is what it should do with its eggs. Shelled eggs, adapted to be in the air or in damp earth at most, are not going to survive in open water, so they must still be laid on land. This means the reptile cannot fully adapt to an aquatic existence—it will always need to be able to move on land, even if in a very limited way. Some aquatic reptiles, though, overcame this in the same way that mammals overcame the need to lay eggs. Their eggs develop inside their bodies, the embryos contained in their amniotic membrane but not in a firm shell, and the young are born when sufficiently developed to swim, just like their parents. Bearing live young, or viviparity, is seen today in the sea snakes, most aquatic of all living reptiles, and also evolved in some Mesozoic groups, such as the lizard-like mosasaurs.

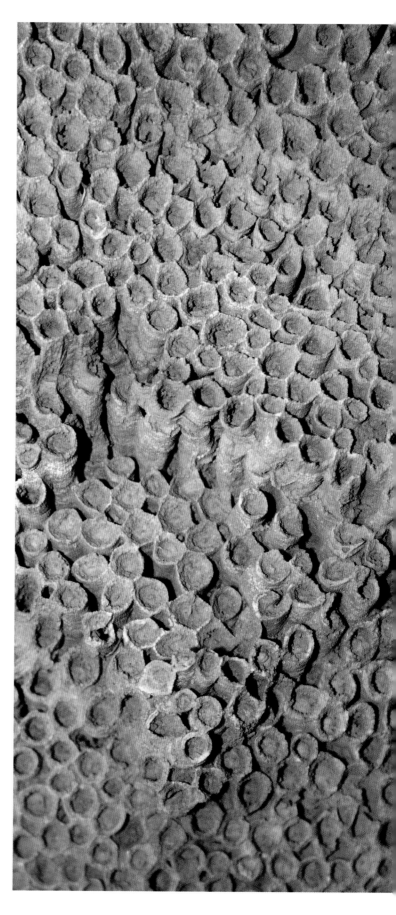

Right *A fossilized rugose coral.*

// Tropical land vertebrates

Above Cynognathus crateronotus *was a powerful, predatory synapsid that lived in the middle Triassic.*

The very early Triassic was a time of high temperatures on land and sea, which was increased further by low sea levels. Pangaea's interior was especially hot (possibly regularly topping 140°F/60°C) and also dry, lacking the rain (from evaporated and then condensed sea water) that would have fallen around coastlines. This would have seriously inhibited the recovery of life in some parts of the world in the first few million years of the Triassic, and in fact 3 million years of steady increase in temperatures brought about a minor extinction event near the start of the Triassic, 249 MYA.

Happily for life on Earth, temperatures had fallen globally to more survivable levels by 247 MYA and now, even in the warmest tropical regions, life began to thrive once again. Vertebrate animals on land—both diapsids and therapsid synapsids—did very well in these environments. Among the widespread groups were the phytosaurs, which were early representatives of the crocodile lineage. Their fossils show that they were very similar to modern true crocodiles, even though they evolved very soon after the ancestors of crocodiles and the ancestors of dinosaurs (including birds) went their separate ways, and more recent crocodile ancestors are in fact less crocodile-like in body shape. Although their name means 'plant-lizards', their array of sharp and serrated teeth shows that they were quite clearly predatory. They were also semi-aquatic, hunting fish and other sizeable prey in and near the water.

The lineage of therapsids that was ancestral to true mammals diversified considerably in the late Triassic. This group, the cynodonts, gave rise to many lineages that did not survive to the end of the Mesozoic, but for the time that they lived, they were nonetheless highly successful. One example is *Cynognathus crateronotus*, whose fossils have been found in southern Africa, Argentina and Antarctica, indicating that it was widespread across Pangaea. It was a predator and resembled a stocky, largeish dog, with robust limbs and head, and a skull that shows crests and ridges for the attachment of strong jaw muscles. The snout of the skull shows large air spaces linked to the mouth and nose, suggesting a strong sensitivity to smells and tactile stimuli (it may have had a whiskered snout).

Another cynodont living in the early Triassic was *Thrinaxodon*, another stocky predator, with a semi-sprawling, lizard-like gait. It probably fed mainly on insects and other small prey. It is one of the earliest of the group to possess a secondary palate in the throat, which separated mouth and nostril airflow, enabling it to continue to breathe while chewing its food. This was an important evolutionary change, improving the efficiency of both digestion and respiration.

ENDOTHERMY

An animal can benefit greatly from the ability to control its internal temperature. Being endothermic allows it to continue being active in both lower and higher temperatures, which gives it more adaptability and enables it to inhabit places that are not accessible to ectothermic animals (which must rely on the ambient temperature falling within certain parameters and are behaviorally limited by temperature factors). Certain land invertebrates have some endothermic ability, but it is land mammals and birds that fully possess this trait. Evidence from fossils suggests that endothermy evolved in the late Permian/early Triassic periods, independently in their two ancestral lineages (archosaurs and synapsids). Endothermy was to serve both groups very well through climatic turbulence in Earth's ongoing history.

Below *The phytosaurs were large water-dwelling archosaurs with a similar body plan and ecology to the crocodiles.*

The first true mammals

Many early Triassic therapsids had a number of mammal-like traits. They had some hair on their skins, they walked with an erect gait, and they could regulate their own body temperature. However, they still laid eggs in large clutches, and the hatchling babies were born with teeth and strong limbs, able to move around freely and find and eat their own food, with no need of a mother's milk.

The lineage of therapsids from which mammals evolved included an early, now-extinct branch known as Docodonta, which existed through the mid-Jurassic until the early Cretaceous Period. These animals were not ancestral to today's mammals but we would certainly recognize them as mammalian, and many palaeontologists classify them as

mammals. They were also highly diverse, occupying many ecological niches that are filled by similar-looking true mammals today—for example, the genus *Castorocauda* was a swimming fish-hunter, like modern otters (though its tail was beaver-like), and *Agiolodocodon* was similar to today's tree shrews. The species *Microdocodon*, a tiny ⅓ oz (9 g) insect-eater, was the earliest of the therapsids to show the distinctive mammal-like hyoid bone in its neck, adapted to allow it to suckle milk.

Another group of early mammals or mammal-like synapsids was the genus *Morganucodon*, known from very widely distributed fossils dating back to the late Triassic. It was small, shrew-like or mouse-like, and its teeth suggested

Below *The widespread genus* Morganucodon *was very like some modern mammal groups, such as the otter shrews of southern Africa.*

Above *Echidna egg. Egg-laying in mammals has all but disappeared in modern groups.*

it enjoyed eating hard-bodied invertebrates, like beetles. Its new-born young lacked teeth, which is strong evidence that they fed on milk. Its fossils also show signs that it had certain skin glands associated with grooming behavior. This implies that it had fur and may also support its having mammary glands (as these glands are modified forms of fat-secreting apocrine glands that open out to the surface of the skin).

The modern mammals that are most basal (closest to the group's shared common ancestor) are the monotremes, represented by the platypus and echidnas. These mammals are egg-layers, unlike all other mammalian species, which give birth to live young. Also, they possess mammary glands but not teats, instead secreting their milk through pores on a bare patch of skin. It is likely that the earliest true mammals showed these same traits, although their fossils show that they had a considerably broader range of shapes, sizes, and lifestyles than those of modern monotremes.

THE NOCTURNAL BOTTLENECK

Early mammals were widespread, often abundant and certainly diverse on Earth through most of the Mesozoic, but fossil evidence indicates that the vast majority shared two fundamental traits—they were small, and they were nocturnal. Most niches suitable for diurnal and larger land vertebrates were occupied by dinosaurs, thus limiting the potential of these early mammals. The nocturnal bottleneck hypothesis suggests that the 160 million years during which early mammals were constrained to a nocturnal lifestyle left a lasting legacy that we see today in typical mammalian traits and behaviors. These include an acute sense of hearing and of smell, large eyes that excel at differentiating contrast but are poorer at discerning color and fine detail, the existence of "brown fat," a tissue that is adapted for heat generation, the tendency to live in burrows, and a circadian rhythm adapted to night-time activity.

// Dispersal through the end of Pangaea

In our modern world, the continents are widely separated. Even for strong-flying birds, a cross-Atlantic or trans-Pacific journey is a major and dangerous undertaking, though not so much for us humans with our myriad means of transport. *Homo sapiens* is the most widespread by far of all large land vertebrates, and this lack of geographical borders that we enjoy is one of the reasons that our population across the planet is remarkably homogenous in genetic terms. However, back in the Triassic when Pangaea was breaking up, this separation of land masses meant that once-homogenous land animal and plant populations would also be broken up into pieces and would probably never reconnect.

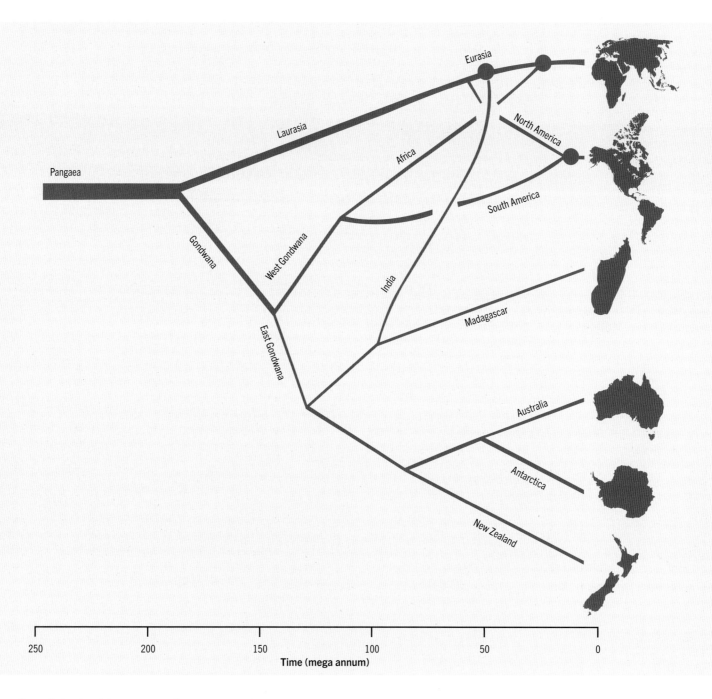

Above *A timeline of the separation of the continents after the break-up of Pangaea.*

Left *Glyptodon is a genus of early armadillos which originated on Gondwana. The largest species topped 4400 lb (2,000 kg), whereas the modern giant armadillo is a lightweight that rarely exceeds 66 lb (30 kg).*

Below *The separation of Gondwanaland from Laurasia, setting into motion the drifting of the continents towards their present-day positions.*

Geographical isolation like this is one of the forces that drives speciation, because conditions will always be different (sometimes very different) on either side of the new geographical boundary. Speciation is the process by which one lineage splits into two—the separated populations become more and more genetically distinct over the generations, as natural selection exerts its influence. To give a simplified example, if one population of a furry mammal is on a land mass drifting north, that population will be under selective pressure to handle longer, darker and colder winters. Later generations are likely to have thicker coats, shorter, more heat-conserving limbs and ears, and may develop a hibernating habit. If the other population drifts south and experiences a hotter climate, the reverse outcome is likely—shorter-furred, lankier animals that are active year-round.

Pangaea's break-up, along with climate changes, caused extensive speciation. It also caused extinctions, as not all species were able to adapt to the changes quickly enough. The initial separation of Laurasia from Gondwanaland created a northern and a southern continent, and the living things on each evolved in different directions, some more successfully than others. The crocodile lineage was present on both continents, but it was the Laurasian population that gave rise to modern crocodiles. Most major modern mammal groups, including carnivores, bats, rodents, primates, and hoofed mammals, also evolved on Laurasia, while on Gondwana, mammals ancestral to modern marsupials, sloths, armadillos,

tenrecs, elephants, and manatees evolved. Back in the Mesozoic, the three major dinosaur groups (theropods, sauropodomorphs and ornithischians) were present on both continents, although two distinct lineages of ornithischians (the armored ankylosaurs and horned psittacosaurs) were confined to the part of Laurasia that would become eastern Asia.

A not-so-mini mass extinction

Towards the end of the Triassic Period, 201.3 MYA, a mass extinction took place. In the palaeontological history books, this event tends to be somewhat overlooked, falling as it does between the colossal losses of the Permian-Triassic event and the later Cretaceous–Paleogene event (K-Pg event), which looms large in our consciousness because it sent all of the dinosaurs (save for the birds) into the pre-history books. However, the Triassic-Jurassic mass extinction event was highly significant in its own right, and in terms of number of species lost, it fell only a little short of the devastation wrought by the K-Pg event.

Like the Permian-Triassic mass extinction, the Triassic-Jurassic event was most likely to have been caused by massive volcanic activity, with all of its dramatic consequences for Earth's climate and weather patterns. In this case, the volcanos were in the Central Atlantic Magmatic Province, an area now mainly under the north Atlantic,

and their eruptions were associated with the separation of Laurasia from Gondwanaland. As with the Siberian Traps eruptions, 50 million years before, release of carbon dioxide caused rapid global warming and oceanic acidification. Some of the animal groups that died out in this event may already have been affected by the climatic aftermath of several meteor strikes over preceding years, including the major strike that formed the 1,207 sq mile (1,942 km^2) Lake Manicouagan in present-day Quebec, Canada.

This mass extinction impacted very heavily on some groups but left others almost unscathed. Ammonites, having survived the Permian-Triassic event, were badly affected, with some families being wiped out. The conodonts, a large group of early fish that were already under pressure from the more recently evolved ray-finned fishes, were wiped out completely. It was not just older marine life forms that were affected, either—the ichthyosaurs, which had diversified

Below *Lake Manicouagan, an impact crater left by a late Triassic meteorite strike in Quebec.*

Left *Fossil conodont teeth.*

into many new forms through the later Triassic, suffered a major drop in diversity. On land, vertebrate diversity was also drastically thinned out, with many large amphibians and members of the crocodile lineage disappearing, along with larger synapsids. The archosaurs, including early dinosaurs, fared better than other vertebrate groups, and the reduction in competition set the stage for them to flourish even more.

Below *This graph shows the diversity of bivalve molluscs over the Triassic and Jurassic periods: before, during, and after the mass extinction.*

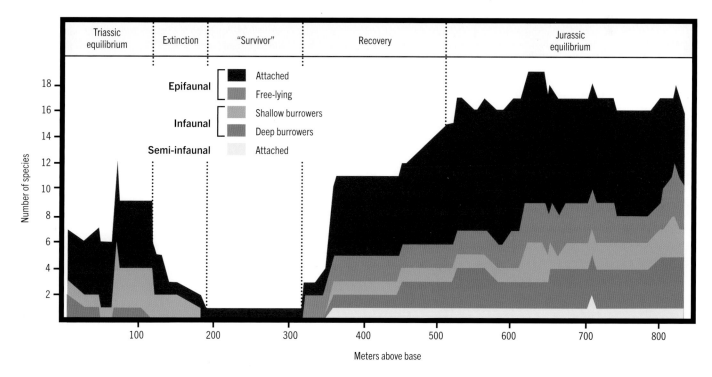

// Gymnosperms—a new way to be a plant

Through the end of the Paleozoic Era, the flora on Earth was changing rapidly. Very tall early plants formed the first forests in Carboniferous times, but then were in competition with the first true trees. The trees we know today that are classified as gymnosperms are more commonly known as pines, spruces, firs, and larches— also sometimes collectively as conifers and evergreens (inaccurately so, because some non-gymnosperm trees also have cones, and many have foliage that remains green and living all year round).

As we have seen, the true distinguishing trait of gymnosperms over the more recently evolved angiosperms is that gymnosperms have exposed seeds (albeit often well sheltered within a cone), while those of angiosperms, or flowering plants, are fully enclosed inside the flower's ovary (later to become a fruit). Reproducing via durable seeds rather than spores gave the gymnosperms an advantage over earlier, spore-bearing plants, especially in more challenging climates, where it could be a long wait for suitable conditions to come about whereby a spore or seed could grow into a new plant. Gymnosperms thrived during the late Paleozoic. Early species, such as the seed ferns, had fully exposed seeds, but the first cone-bearing species appeared late in the Carboniferous Period.

In the Mesozoic, new lineages of gymnosperms appeared, some of which were destined to stay the course and survive into modern times. The first tree considered a true pine (genus *Pinus*) lived some 140 MYA, in the late Jurassic. The cypress lineage also emerged in the Jurassic, while the small and shrubby or climbing gnetophytes (whose modern relatives include the bizarre huge-leaved desert shrub *Welwitschia*) may have evolved as early as the Permian.

THE ORIGIN OF SEX

Coniferous gymnosperms offer an obvious example of sexual reproduction—the formation of new individuals by combining genes from two different parents. Wind carries pollen grains, containing male gametes, away from pollen sacs on specialized leaves. Some of these end up making contact with female gametes, held within the seeds inside the cones. Most gymnosperms produce both male and female gametes but avoid self-fertilizing by various means, including opening the pollen sacs and cones at different times. We often think of sexual reproduction as being a relatively recent evolutionary phenomenon, but in fact eukaryotes have been reproducing this way (as well as by asexual methods such as budding) for about as long as they have existed, and even bacteria engage in forms of sexual reproduction, by exchanging pieces of genetic material with other individuals.

Below *Sexual reproduction in cone-bearing gymnosperms.*

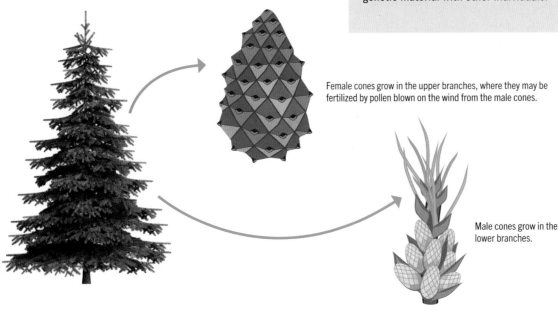

Female cones grow in the upper branches, where they may be fertilized by pollen blown on the wind from the male cones.

Male cones grow in the lower branches.

Left *Many forests in northern temperate zones today are composed primarily of gymnosperm trees such as pines.*

Below Welwitschia, *one of the few living descendants of the gnetophyte lineage that first appeared during the Permian period.*

// Dinosaurs—the sauropods

Of all the famous dinosaurs that we learn about from an early age, few command our awe as much as the giant sauropods. No wonder—for they are far larger than any land animal alive today, or indeed that ever lived in the whole history of our planet. With so much tonnage, adult sauropods of the biggest species had little to fear from even the most sizeable predatory dinosaurs, and so could pursue a relatively leisurely life, moving slowly between places to eat, drink, and rest, and feeding only on vegetation.

Because of our own evolutionary history, we tend to think of walking on two legs as being a progression from four, but the sauropods actually descend from bipedal (and

small) ancestors. Sauropods and their direct ancestors are collectively known as sauropodomorphs, but only the four-legged giants are sauropods. Several different lineages independently grew larger over countless generations, and as their size increased their forelimbs also became weight-bearing, though the center of gravity still tended towards the rear of the body and some were still comfortable standing on their hind legs (perhaps to reach higher foliage), using the tail for additional support. The four strong, upright (rather than sideways-sprawling) limbs supported a hefty but relatively short body, plus the extremely long neck and tail. The very smallest sauropods were still at least 13.1 ft (4 m) long from nose to tail-tip, and the longest (*Argentinosaurus*) could have grown to 114.8 ft (35 m) long and tipped the scales at as much as 78.7 US tons (80 tonnes). Their relatively small heads were equipped with tough leaf-grinding teeth that wore down and were replaced in as little as 14 days per tooth.

For their size, sauropods were not actually as heavy as they might have been because, like some other dinosaurs and also modern birds, their bodies contained a system of air sacs that connected to the lungs. This would have given them buoyancy when foraging in water, which they appear to have done regularly (many fossil finds are associated with wetland and coastal habitats), though they would have been comfortable moving on dry land too. Fossils and trackways also suggest that these were highly social animals, living in herds and, in some cases, showing signs of long-term parental care with juveniles associating with adults for long periods.

The first fossils recognized as true sauropods date back to the very late Triassic and early Jurassic, with the group reaching its greatest diversity in the late Jurassic. Many lineages survived well into the Cretaceous, but toward the end of the Cretaceous only one lineage remained. These were the enormous titanosaurs, including *Argentinosaurus*, plus the armored and short-necked *Saltasaurus*. These species existed up until the mass extinction that took place at the end of the Cretaceous, but many other well-known sauropods, such as *Diplodocus* and *Brontosaurus*, were already long extinct by this time.

DIPPY

The Natural History Museum in London was home for more than 100 years to a 85.3 ft (26 m) replica *Diplodocus carnegii* skeleton, based on fossil bones that are now on display at the Carnegie Museum of Natural History in Pittsburgh. The replica, known as 'Dippy', started out in the reptile gallery but became the much-loved centerpiece in the museum's main hall from 1979 until 2017. Since then, it has toured a number of other UK museums and galleries.

Left *"Dippy" the* Diplodocus *model, on display in Glasgow's Kelvingrove Art Gallery and Museum.*

// Dinosaurs—early meat-eating bipeds

The very early saurischian dinosaurs of Triassic times were bipedal and mainly small in size. They included a family called Herrerasauridae, which lived from the late Triassic until the Triassic-Jurassic mass extinction. They show some traits suggestive of sauropodomorphs and others that are more similar to theropods, though are not thought to be directly ancestral to either group. Other basal saurischians that were probably in the theropod lineage included the robust, sharp-toothed little *Daemonosaurus*, and the slim and dainty 8.2ft (2.5m) *Tawa*. One of the earliest ever was the chicken-sized *Pendraig milnerae*, which lived about 210 MYA and was, despite its small stature, probably one of the top predators in its environment.

By the early Jurassic, the first definite members of the theropod lineage were widespread on Earth and included some much larger species. The group known as Coelophysoidea were highly successful. These rather dainty, fast-running hunters were up to 19.7ft (6 m) long and may have lived and hunted in packs, allowing them to tackle larger prey. Some even bigger and more robust theropods had also evolved by this time, among them the genus *Saltriovenator*, which probably reached 26.2 ft (8 m) in length. It is the oldest known member of the group Ceratosauria, which includes the three-horned, small-armed *Ceratosaurus* of the late Jurassic.

Below *A formidable Jurassic predator,* Ceratosaurus *was between 18–23 ft (5.5–7 m) in length.*

These early theropods were mainly fast-running predators, which would have hunted other dinosaurs as well as mammals and other reptiles. Some seized prey with their forelimbs, which often had large and powerful claws, while others developed larger heads with stronger jaws, using these instead to catch their food. As the Jurassic progressed, some theropod lineages grew larger still, the better to hunt the similarly sizeable herbivores that were also evolving at that time, but very small theropods also existed throughout the Mesozoic. Some of these small species became specialized insect-eaters, while others evolved over time to become omnivorous or even mainly herbivorous.

BIRD HIPS AND LIZARD HIPS

As we have seen, dinosaurs belong to one of three groups—the sauropodomorphs, the theropods, and the ornithischians. The most fundamental breakdown of dinosaur ancestry, though, shows just two original lineages—Saurischia ("lizard-hipped") and Ornithischia ("bird-hipped"). Of the three main dinosaur lineages, two (the sauropodomorphs and theropods) are branches of Saurischia, with only the third (the ornithischians) belonging to Ornithischia. It is rather counter-intuitive that the theropod dinosaurs that gave rise to actual birds are "lizard-hipped" and not "bird-hipped." However, evolution has reshaped the modern bird pelvis to become more similar to the ornithischians than that of their theropod ancestors.

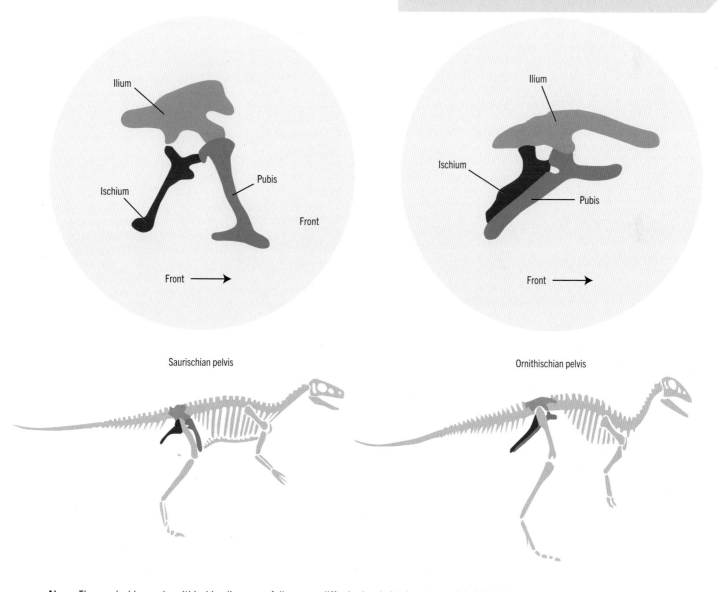

Saurischian pelvis

Ornithischian pelvis

Above *The saurischian and ornithischian lineages of dinosaurs differ in the skeletal anatomy of their hip joints.*

// Dinosaurs—Stegosaurus and other ornithischians

One of the most iconic portrayals of dinosaur life can be found in Disney's 1940s highly theatrical animation *Fantasia*. In a long sequence covering our planet's prehistory, set to Stravinsky's *The Rite of Spring*, a *Stegosaurus* and a *Tyrannosaurus* battle to the death, the armored herbivore eventually and inevitably succumbing to the great theropod's deadly jaws. This thrilling scene has undoubtedly contributed toward *Stegosaurus* becoming one of the most instantly recognizable dinosaurs, even though the fight could never have occurred in nature, as *Stegosaurus* had been extinct for more than 70 million years before *Tyrannosaurus* first appears in the fossil record.

The "bird-hipped" ornithischian dinosaurs were a diverse group in appearance and anatomy, and the heavy-set and mighty *Stegosaurus* was one of the least "bird-like" of them all. The largest species within the genus were at least 23 ft (7 m) long and weighed nearly 4.4 US tons (4 tonnes). They were herbivores, but well protected from would-be attackers by the spiked tail-tip that would have functioned like a mace. The distinctive double row of bony plates along their spines are thought to have helped them to regulate their body temperature, providing a large surface area through which heat could be lost or absorbed as needed.

Below Iguanadon *was a hefty quadrupedal dinosaur, but belonged to the "bird-hipped" lineage—its tracks were also rather bird-like.*

Above *The bony plates on Stegosaurus's back would have given it some protection from large predators.*

As well as armored dinosaurs like *Stegosaurus*, Jurassic-Era ornithischians included *Iguanodon*, a genus of relatively short-legged, heavy-duty herbivores that were originally interpreted as having walked on four legs. However, they also show signs of having been able to manipulate items with their forelimbs, so may have been at least partly bipedal. *Iguanodon* is part of the ornithischian group Ornithopoda— the "bird-footed" dinosaurs. Another Jurassic representative of this group is *Heterodontosaurus*, a name meaning "lizard with different teeth" because its snub-nosed skull features a jaw lined with chunky grinding teeth suggestive of an herbivorous diet, but with large pointed "tusks" and sharp incisors at the front. This was a small bipedal dinosaur with a beaked face, which may have used its strong forelimbs to dig

up roots and other foods. It was also probably a fast runner, which would have helped it to escape danger. Its tusks may have been used in dominance contests rather than for feeding or predator defense, but their function is not known for certain.

Heterodontosaurus shared its habitat and timespan with the larger *Lesothosaurus*. This graceful and small-armed biped is one of the most basal ornithischians, lacking any specialized features such as the spiked tail and bony plates of *Stegosaurus,* or the peculiar teeth of *Heterodontosaurus*. Indeed, fossil remains of its unspecialized teeth do not show the wear pattern typical of a plant-eater, so *Lesothosaurus* may have been an omnivore.

// An explosion of mammal diversity

One of the great theropod predators of the Jurassic, *Megalosaurus*, is well known from fossil finds that date back to 166 MYA. This 26.2 ft (8 m)-long, huge-jawed biped was one of the first dinosaurs to be described in scientific literature, from a fragment of femur found in the 17th century. Other *Megalosaurus* fossils, found in an Oxfordshire quarry, were much studied by the naturalist William Buckland in the 19th century. The same fossil deposit also yielded some mammalian remains—at the time, these were the first mammal fossils known from the era.

This mammal, still only known from the jaws and teeth found in that quarry, was named *Phascolotherium*, and classified in the group Eutriconodonta, a group of early egg-laying mammals that were widespread in the second half of the Mesozoic. In stark contrast to the huge bones of *Megalosaurus*, the *Phascolotherium* jaws were miniscule, just 1.3 in (3.3 cm) long. The picture thus created in human minds was of gigantic reptiles stomping through the Jurassic landscape, while a handful of tiny furry beasts lived in the dinosaurs' shadows and did their best to stay out of their way. However, subsequent discoveries have shown

Below *The tiny lower jaw of* Plascolotherium, *a Jurassic mammal.*

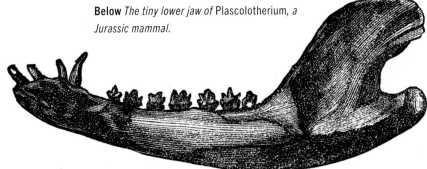

Below *The mighty* Megalosaurus *was a dominant Mesozoic predator across what is now southern England.*

that the Jurassic was actually a great time for mammals, with diversity and abundance increasing rapidly—though none of these mammals reached anything like the body sizes attained by the bigger dinosaurs.

The eutriconodonts, or "trikes" as they are affectionately nicknamed by some palaeontologists, provide prime examples of this impressive diversity. Many of the forms that evolved are strikingly similar to unrelated modern mammals, showing how certain innovations seem to occur again and again through evolutionary history. For example, the genus *Volaticotherium* had skin membranes stretching between its forefeet and hind feet, allowing it to leap and then glide, as flying squirrels and sugar gliders do today. The aquatic genus *Liaoconodon* would have put us in mind of modern otters, with its long, low-slung body and broad feet. *Fruitafossor* had strong digging limbs and resembled an armadillo. Many other eutriconodonts resembled modern shrews or tree shrews.

Below *Diagram of reptile and mammal skulls showing repurposing of bones for mammalian middle ear.*

SOUNDS LIKE A MAMMAL?

As we have seen, modern mammals are a lineage of a certain group of reptiles—the therapsids. Today, we have no difficulty telling what we call mammals from what we call reptiles, based on a wide range of traits. Mammals feed their young on milk, fully control their own body temperature, and grow hair or fur on their skins—reptiles do none of these things. However, we would have a much harder time classifying various therapsids as mammal or reptile if they were alive today. The changes from producing self-sufficient young to milk-dependent young, ectothermic to endothermic bodies, and scaly to hairy skin occurred independently and at different rates. One of the traits that is sometimes used as a simple differentiator on its own is the anatomy of the jawbones—in mammals, three small bones of the reptilian jaw have shifted to become part of the middle ear. Here, these bones (the malleus, incus and stapes, collectively known as the ossicles) function to conduct sound waves. This trait is easier to find in fossils than features indicative of functions such as lactation and thermoregulation.

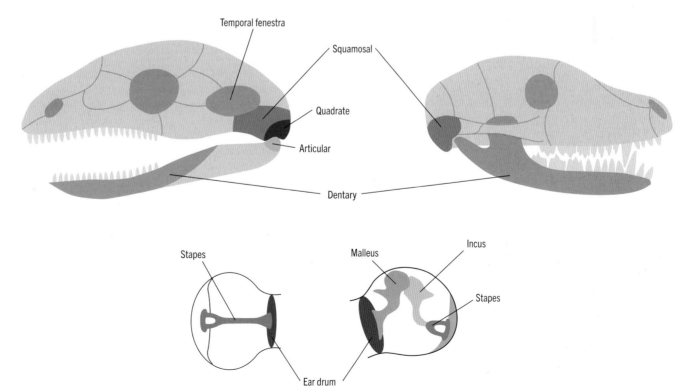

Diagram of a reptile skull and middle ear

Temporal fenestra
Squamosal
Quadrate
Articular
Dentary
Stapes
Ear drum

Diagram of a mammal skull and middle ear

Incus
Malleus
Stapes

// Marine giants—plesiosaurs and more

The not-entirely-scientific field of cryptozoology concerns animals that may not exist. This is the domain of Bigfoot, yetis and black panthers at large in countries where leopards and jaguars do not naturally occur. Often the stars of local legend, these animals leave ambiguous signs of their presence, and can never be clearly photographed. One of the best-known cryptids of all is the Loch Ness Monster, or "Nessie"—unverified inhabitant of one of Scotland's deepest glacial lakes. Although there is, as yet, no evidence that Nessie herself exists, the animals that most resemble descriptions of her certainly did once dwell in the lochs and oceans of their time.

The plesiosaurs were large marine reptiles with long slender necks, flattened tails, and limbs modified into long flippers, like those of modern sea turtles. They swam at a leisurely pace using these flippers and by beating their tails up and down, and preyed on fish and other small aquatic animals. They, along with other great marine reptiles of the late Paleozoic and the Mesozoic, descend from land-dwelling reptiles, but are not dinosaurs, their direct ancestors having diverged from a shared lineage long before the first dinosaurs appeared.

Above *The long-necked plesiosaurs were vaguely similar to sauropod dinosaurs but built for swimming rather than walking.*

Below *Loch Ness in Scotland—long rumored to be home to an anachronistic solitary plesiosaur.*

Above *A pliosaur fossil found by Mary Anning.*

The pliosaurs were close cousins of the plesiosaurs—together they formed the group Plesiosauria. However, they had strikingly different morphology, as they were adapted to a different way of life. If plesiosaurs resembled sea-going sauropods, the pliosaurs could be likened to modern orcas or flipper-footed crocodiles—large but short-necked, short-tailed and big-headed swimmers that swam quickly and took down much bigger prey relative to their own body size.

A third group of large marine reptiles showed the most dramatic adaptation of all to their watery habitat, even though they, too, descended from land-dwelling ancestors. The ichthyosaurs first appeared in the early Triassic and thrived through the Jurassic, though they appear to have been outcompeted by plesiosaurs and pliosaurs later in the Mesozoic. The morphology of many ichthyosaurs was extremely fish-like, with a neckless, streamlined body, vertically flattened and finned tail, a dorsal fin and fin-like hind and forelimbs (the hind limbs being much reduced in size in some species). The jaws were long and beak-like, with numerous sharp teeth.

MARY ANNING

One of the most notable fossil finds of a long-extinct marine reptile came courtesy of a 12-year-old girl, Mary Anning. She discovered the skeleton of what turned out to be the ichthyosaur *Temnodontosaurus platyodon* embedded in the fossil-rich cliffs of south Dorset, UK, in around 1810. Her passion for palaeontology lasted a lifetime and she found several more ichthyosaurs, along with plesiosaur skeletons and other important Mesozoic fossils. The scientists who prepared descriptions of her early finds often left her name entirely out of their writings, and it was many decades after her death (at just 47) before her importance and impact on palaeontological science was properly recognized and credited.

The first eutherian mammals

Modern mammals form three groups—the monotremes, the metatherians (marsupials and their immediate ancestors), and the placental mammals and their immediate ancestors, known collectively as eutherians. The great majority of mammals living today are eutherians, with all extant monotremes and most extant marsupials only occurring in places that have very few eutherians. The monotremes, represented today by the platypus and four species of echidna, are the world's only egg-laying mammals, and they and their extinct relatives are known as prototherians. Their ancestors split from other mammal lineages some 220 MYA. The separation of metatherians from eutherians, though, was much more recent. And, although all modern eutherians are placental mammals, early prehistoric eutherians are not considered to be true placental mammals.

The oldest known eutherian fossil is of an animal that lived in what is now China, in the late Jurassic about 161 MYA. This animal, *Juramaia*, was a small tree-dwelling mammal that fed on insects and other invertebrates—in appearance and lifestyle it was similar to modern shrews. It can be inferred that metatherians also existed at this time, but there are currently no known metatherian fossils as old as *Juramaia*. Another early eutherian was *Eomaia*, which lived some 125 MYA. It was another small, climbing species but was a little more robust than *Juramaia*. Neither *Eomaia* nor *Juramaia* show all the signs of being true placental mammals—in particular, their pelvic anatomy suggests they gave birth to small, undeveloped young, so probably did not have placentas.

The tiny *Sinodelphys* is another early eutherian, 125 million years old, which is known from a single but very well preserved complete skeleton recovered fron the Yixian Formation in Liaoning Province, China. Imprints left by the animal's hair and some of its soft tissue are visible around the fossilized bones. The same fossil beds have yielded a range of other early Cretaceous mammals, including *Sinobaatar*,

a plant-eater belonging to the group Multituberculata. This group, now entirely extinct, has traits in common with both metatherians and eutherians but is not considered to be ancestral to either of them, and is classed as prototherian. Although Multituberculata did not reach modern times, it did survive the Cretaceous-Paleogene mass extinction and indeed became very diverse and numerous through the early Paleogene, giving rise to an array of forms, including the 220 lb (100 kg) *Taeniolabis*, but multituberculates were eventually outcompeted by eutherian mammals.

Above *The Tasmanian Devil, along with its fellow Australian marsupials, is a modern-day representative of the group Metatheria.*

COUNTING OUT THE TEETH

The most obvious distinction between metatherians and eutherians today is that metatherians have brief pregnancies and give birth to embryonic offspring, which are then nourished on milk within their mother's pouch for an extended period. Eutherian offspring remain in the mother's uterus for a longer period and are nourished via a placenta, so are born after a longer gestation and in a more developed state. This distinction is not readily inferred from skeletal fossils, but luckily for palaeontologists, the two groups also have reliably different teeth (metatherians always have four sets of molars, while eutherians always have a maximum of three sets).

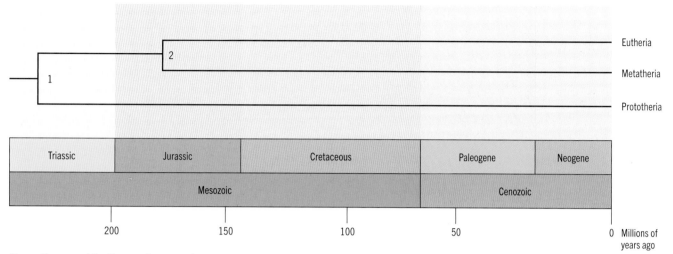

Above *Lineages of the three main mammal groups.*

Below *Fossil of the rodent-like* Sinobaatar, *an early Cretaceous member of the diverse order Multituberculata.*

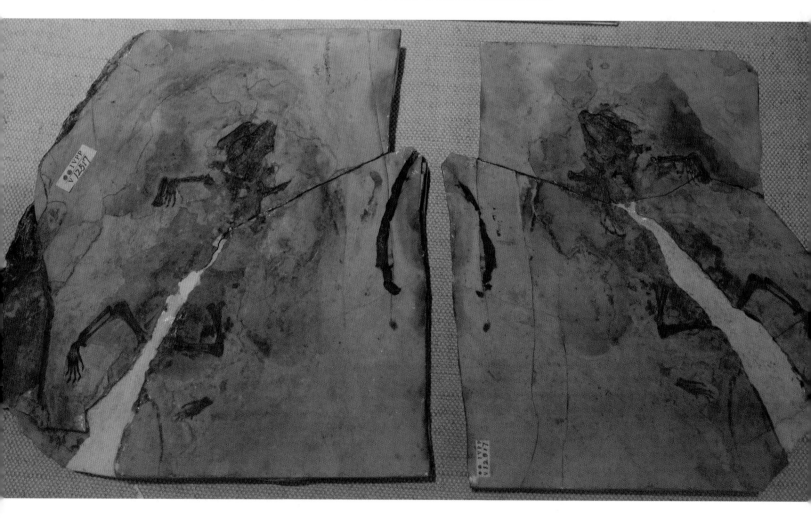

// Jurassic dark—extinctions in the mid-Mesozoic

The longest period in our planet's history between mass extinction events took place in the Mesozoic. About 135 million years elapsed between the Triassic-Jurassic event and the Cretaceous-Paleogene event, and during the earlier part of this time in particular, the background extinction rate was also considerably lower than at other times. Our planet was becoming generally more hospitable to a wide variety of living things, thanks to the break-up of Pangaea, wirhmost land masses and shallow seas enjoying a warm climate and (until the very end of the era) no serious extra-terrestrial impacts. Nevertheless, 135 million years is a very long time and, with the average lifespan of a species being only about 1 million years, there were inevitably many extinctions of species, genera, and larger groups.

As we have already seen, the iconic dinosaur *Stegosaurus* died out in the Jurassic. Many other dinosaur groups met a similar fate, among them the well-known theropod *Allosaurus*. This large and fearsome dinosaur was the alpha predator in its environment and would have hunted *Stegosaurus* along with juveniles of the large sauropods living at the time. Many of the best-known sauropods also met their ends during the Jurassic—among them *Diplodocus*, *Brachiosaurus,* and the very robust and heavy *Apatosaurus*.

Below Allosaurus, *a predator seen by many dinosaur enthusiasts as a spiritual predecessor to* Tyrannosaurus, *died out in the Jurassic period.*

Above *One of the world's most striking examples of convergent evolution, the fish-like but reptilian ichthyosaurs died out in the Cretaceous period.*

Right *Kayentatherium, a mammal-like tritylodont lived in the area we now know as northern Arizona, USA.*

The early Cretaceous saw the demise of the tritylodontids, which were the very last non-mammalian synapsids. Although they were not considered to be mammals, they did have furry coats and a mammal-like stance. Their heavy-duty molars and strong jaws suggest that these proto-mammals were plant-eaters, although in appearance they were more similar to modern weasels and martens. The advent and tremendous rise of the flowering plants had an impact on other plant groups, with the bennettitales (a group of cycad-like gymnosperms) being among those that disappeared completely. Some insect groups were also lost, among them the dragonfly-like Tarsophlebioptera and the diverse early moth family Eolepitopterigidae.

Turning to the seas, the ichthyosaurs died out completely 90 MYA, well before the Cretaceous-Paleogene event that finished off the plesiosaurs. It is thought that they were less able to cope with the climate changes that began in the mid-Cretaceous than were their fellow marine reptiles. Many bivalve molluscs also died out in the mid-Jurassic Period, as did a large number of ammonite species and genera, paving the way for the ammonites' swan song at the Cretaceous-Paleogene mass extinction event.

The rise of sharks and rays

Although bony fish have dominated the Earth's fishy landscapes since before the Mesozoic began, the Jurassic Period saw a great radiation of cartilaginous fish—the sharks, rays, and related species. This group had already been highly successful during the Devonian and Carboniferous Periods, spawning such remarkable groups as the large-finned, "flying" iniopterygians and the scissor-toothed *Edestus*. However, their numbers were dramatically thinned out in the Permian mass extinction. Nevertheless, several groups survived, and as the Mesozoic progressed, they became much more diverse once again. It was in the Jurassic that modern shark and ray families first emerged.

Through the Mesozoic Era, sharks lived in both marine and freshwater environments. One of the groups that frequented the latter was the xenacanths, which were rather small, elongated, and eel-like, and carried a strange backward-pointing spine on their heads. They remain today the most successful of all freshwater shark lineages through Earth's history, although they did not survive long into the Mesozoic. The group known as hydobonts, which had distinctive cone-shaped teeth, a double dorsal fin, and (in males) a spine-covered head, also included some freshwater species, and some of these sharks survived up until the Cretaceous-Paleogene mass extinction. The family Mitsukurinidae was once a fairly diverse group of deep-sea sharks that lived in the late Mesozoic, and today has a single living representative in the form of the bizarre goblin shark with its pink skin, elongated snout (covered in sensory organs that can detect electrical fields generated by nearby prey), and protrusible jaws.

Rays that resemble modern species first emerged in the Jurassic, including *Antiquaobatis* and *Spathobatis*, both of which had the characteristic wide and flattened body, with eyes on top and mouth on the underside. Like many modern rays, these species probably rested and foraged on the seabed. Sawfish, a peculiar subgroup of rays notable for their very large size (up to 23 ft/7 m long) and long rostrum or snout, lined with sharp "teeth" like a hand saw, probably first emerged at the very end of the Mesozoic.

Below *The goblin shark is a curious modern-day relic from a once diverse Mesozoic family.*

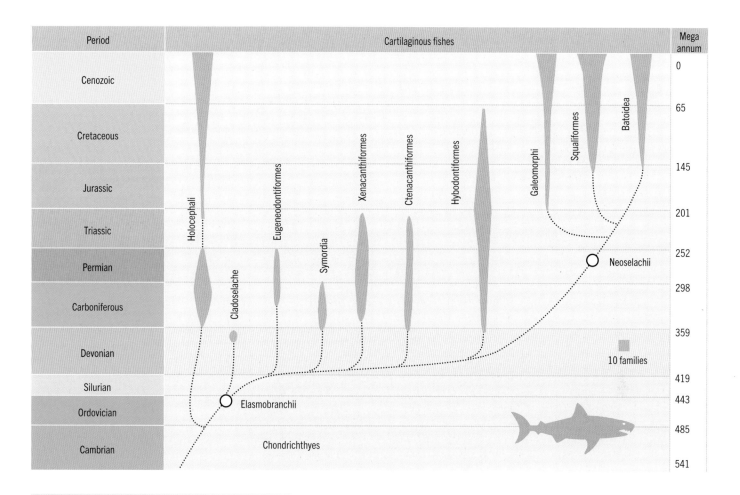

Period	Cartilaginous fishes	Mega annum
Cenozoic		0
Cretaceous		65
Jurassic		145
Triassic		201
Permian		252
Carboniferous		298
Devonian		359
Silurian		419
Ordovician		443
Cambrian		485
		541

Holocephali · Cladoselache · Eugeneodontiformes · Symordia · Xenacanthiformes · Ctenacanthiformes · Hybodontiformes · Galeomorphi · Squaliformes · Batoidea · Neoselachii · Elasmobranchii · Chondrichthyes · 10 families

CHIMAERAS

Almost all modern cartilaginous fish fall within a grouping known as Elasmobranchii. This category includes all living and extinct sharks, rays, skates, and sawfish. The only living cartilaginous fish that fall outside this grouping are the chimaeras—big-headed deep-sea fishes that are vaguely shark-like in appearance and are sometimes known as "ghost sharks." The chimaera lineage is far more ancient than that of any living shark or ray, as true chimaeras first emerged way back in the Cambrian or Silurian Period, in the early Paleozoic. By the Carboniferous Period, chimaeras were highly diverse, but unlike many other cartilaginous fish groups around at that time, they managed to survive the Permian mass extinction. They did not attain their former diversity through the Mesozoic or Cenozoic, but a few species have persisted to modern times.

Above *The evolutionary timeline of sharks, rays, and related species. Several new lineages emerged in the Mesozoic.*

Below *The most obscure of the cartilaginous fish lineages, the chimaeras can trace their ancestry back well over 500 million years.*

// Modern insect groups appear

Relatively few lineages of invertebrate animals have made a success of life on dry land. Insects, though, eclipse all the rest, with 1 million described species and many more still awaiting discovery. They thrived first in the mid-Paleozoic when a land surface covered with eatable plants and an atmosphere rich in oxygen created perfect conditions for them to spread and diversify—especially once they evolved the power of flight. They were severely affected by the Permian mass extinction, but the Mesozoic saw a dramatic bounce-back, with the appearance of many of the 24 main groupings or orders of insects that live today.

Of these 24 orders, four are particularly species-rich. These are Coleoptera (the beetles), Lepidoptera (butterflies and moths), Hymenoptera (bees, wasps, ants, and sawflies), and Diptera (the true flies, which include hoverflies, mosquitoes, and craneflies. All four of these belong to the subgroup Endopterygota. These are insects that have four life stages—egg, larva (which grows larger through successive molts), pupa, and finally adult. The other, more primitive insect subgroup, Exopterygota, has no pupa stage—instead the larvae gradually become more adult-like after each molt, until reaching full adulthood after the final molt.

Beetles first appeared just prior to the Mesozoic, but their diversity increased at a staggering rate during the Jurassic, with the first weevils, scarab beetles, click beetles, and jewel beetles dating back to this time. The first members of Hymenoptera to appear in the fossil record were the big-winged sawflies of the family Xyelidae, which appeared in the Triassic. This family survives today, represented by a few species found in northern pine forests. The first parasitic wasps evolved in the Jurassic Period, while in the Cretaceous Period the earliest bees and social wasps appeared.

The butterflies and moths diverged from their closest relatives, the caddisflies, in the Triassic, and a few clearly lepidopteran fossils have been described from later in the Mesozoic, although these insects tend to be preserved very poorly due to their fragile bodies and their preference for non-watery habitats where fossilization processes are less likely to occur. True flies first appeared in the mid-Triassic, branching off from a lineage that also included scorpionflies and fleas.

LIQUID LUNCH

In their adult forms, butterflies and moths and the true flies have mouthparts adapted for sucking up liquids. Today, most butterflies and moths and a substantial number of true flies depend on the nectar produced by flowering plants, but without this food source they would have fed on other liquids. As most of us know to our chagrin, some flies dine on vertebrate blood. Another source of nutritious liquids that both of these groups still exploit are the sweet secretions or honeydew produced by sap-sucking insects of the order Hemiptera (the "true bugs"). As Hemiptera evolved back in the Carboniferous, this food supply could have sustained Mesozoic butterflies, moths, and flies prior to the evolution of flowering plants.

Below *Fossilized insect of the Mesozoic family Kalligrammatidae, which resembled moths but were actually lacewings.*

Opposite *An ant "milks" its herd of aphids for their honeydew secretions. Ants have lived on Earth for 100 million years.*

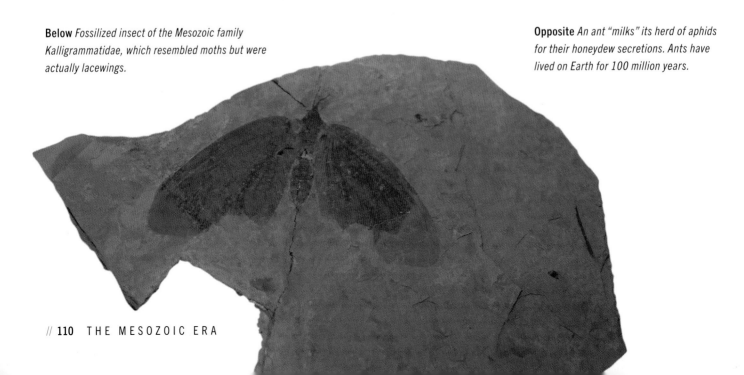

// Octopuses and other sea invertebrates

Our notions about invertebrate animals being self-evidently less evolved, less intelligent, and just generally lesser than their vertebrate cousins are today being challenged like never before. The animals responsible for this re-examination of our old prejudices are the octopuses and their fellow cephalopods—squids, cuttlefish, and nautiluses. Belonging to the phylum Mollusca, these big-brained, tentacled creatures are related to clams and cockles, but could scarcely be more different to them in terms of the way they live. We now know that many cephalopods are fast and inventive learners and adept problem-solvers, as well as showing sophisticated social behavior.

The earliest cephalopod fossils date back to the late Cambrian Period, with the first of the shell-less coleoids (the group that includes modern octopuses, squids, and cuttlefish) emerging in the Carboniferous Period. Cephalopods thrived up until the end of the Paleozoic, but were almost completely obliterated in the Permian mass extinction. The handful of survivors, though, gave rise to a spectacular radiation of new species as the Mesozoic progressed and coastal waters became more cephalopod-friendly.

Mesozoic oceans were home to many other invertebrate groups, living alongside the great reptiles that had returned to the waters following a spell of evolution as land-dwellers. Other molluscs thrived in this time, and the ammonites also fared well. Marine arthropods, in particular crabs, lobsters and other crustaceans, also thrived. The mysterious Thylacocephala, which survived into the Cretaceous Period, was a peculiar group of possible crustaceans that had a two-fold carapace, numerous swimming legs and three pairs of large prey-seizing appendages, and enormous, complex compound eyes. The echinoderms, which include starfish, brittle stars, crinoids, and sea urchins, were also abundant and diverse during the middle Mesozoic, despite also suffering near complete extinction at the end of the Permian.

GAMING THE SYSTEM

As we have seen, the usual pathway of evolutionary change takes as its starting point a population of individual organisms with different traits. Natural selection "picks off" those individuals whose traits make them less well adapted to survival, leaving the best-adapted to survive and procreate, passing on their favorable traits. The variation in traits comes down to random mutations in the organisms' DNA—the genetic material that resides in each cell nucleus and carries the code for how to build all the proteins that make up their bodies. The DNA is transcribed into RNA strands, which go out into the cell and actually build the proteins. However, recent research has revealed that squids and octopuses have been found to regularly change the proteins they build by "editing" their RNA, rather than through DNA mutation. This process, which is very rare in other living things, implies that very high innate adaptability exists in cephalopods, and also indicates that cephalopod evolution via the "usual route" may have been far slower than we would otherwise expect.

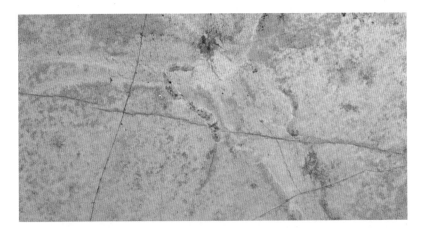

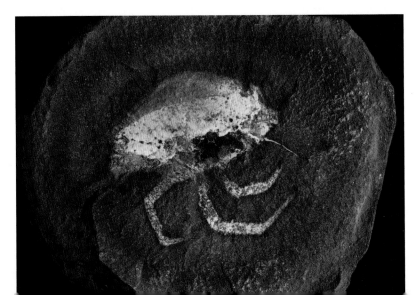

Above right *Less well known than the related ammonites, the squid-like belemnoids died out at the end of the Cretaceous.*

Below right *A fossil thylacocephalan or "flea shrimp."*

Opposite *Cephalopod evolutionary tree.*

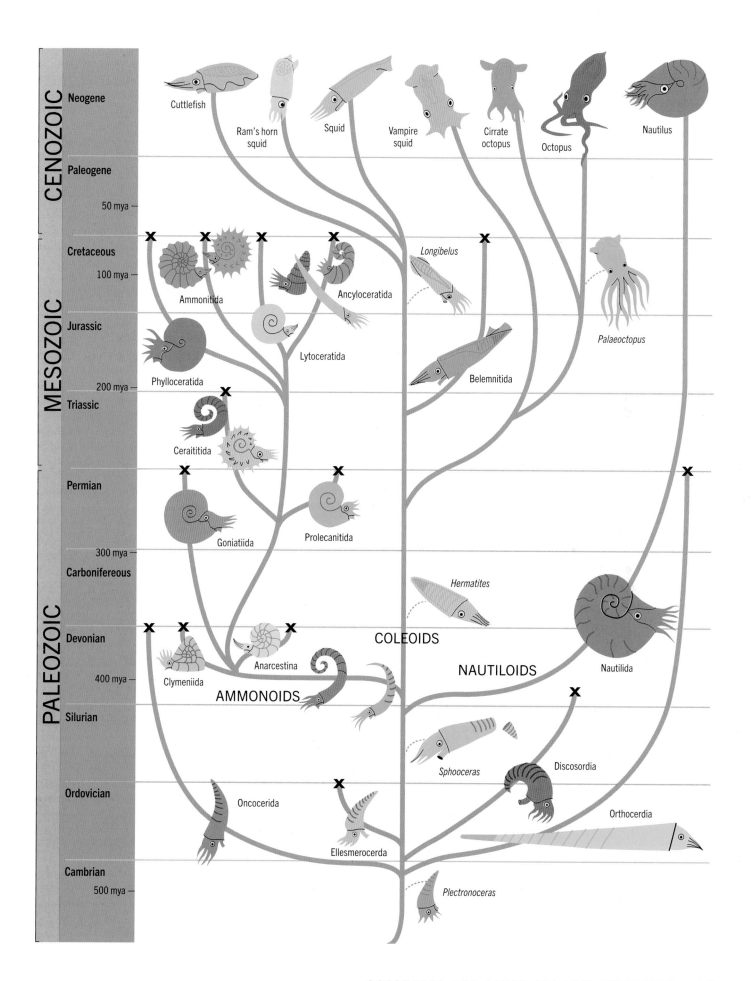

Cuttlefish

Ram's horn squid

Squid

Vampire squid

Cirrate octopus

Octopus

Nautilus

Longibelus

Ammonitida

Ancyloceratida

Lytoceratida

Belemnitida

Palaeoctopus

Phylloceratida

Ceraititida

Goniatiida

Prolecanitida

Hermatites

Clymeniida

Anarcestina

COLEOIDS

NAUTILOIDS

Nautilida

AMMONOIDS

Sphooceras

Discosordia

Oncocerida

Ellesmerocerda

Orthocerdia

Cambrian

Plectronoceras

CENOZOIC

Neogene

Paleogene

50 mya —

MESOZOIC

Cretaceous

100 mya —

Jurassic

200 mya —

Triassic

PALEOZOIC

Permian

300 mya —

Carbonifereous

Devonian

400 mya —

Silurian

Ordovician

500 mya —

// The first flowering plants

We humans love flowers, for their diversity in form, beauty in color and pattern, and their sweet scents. In some cases, we also love what the flowers become once their petals fall—sweet and succulent fruits. Evolution has indeed shaped many flowers and fruits to appeal—on many levels—to animals like us, and the symbiotic relationships between flowering plants (or angiosperms) and their pollinators and seed-dispersers, dating back to Mesozoic times, have resulted in some of the true modern wonders of the natural world.

Gymnosperms—which bear unenclosed seeds rather than spores—evolved in the Paleozoic, and at the very end of this era the gymnosperm lineage had given rise to the ancestors of angiosperms, which were characterized by their enclosed seeds. Some fossilized Jurassic plants, such as *Nanjinganthus*, show certain angiosperm-like traits. However, the earliest signs of true angiosperms do not appear in the fossil record until the early Cretaceous. Once they did appear on the scene, though, they thrived and spread at a dramatic rate, and competed very successfully against the gymnosperms and other, simpler plants already present at the time. One of the keys to angiosperm success was a shorter genome (the sum total of all the DNA held in each cell's nucleus) compared to gymnosperms. This meant that the actual cells making up the plant's foliage could be smaller, which made for more efficient photosynthesis and respiration, and faster growth.

The small, petal-less flower *Micropetasos*, found preserved in 100-million-year-old amber in Burma in the early 2000s, showed evidence of having been pollinated by insects—there were sticky pollen grains on the flowers' stigmas (female reproductive parts). The pollen's stickiness strongly suggests that it was carried by insects rather than on the wind. In addition to the flowers, the amber deposits also contained some preserved insects, including the bee *Melittosphex burmensis* which, at just shy of 0.12 in (3 mm) long, would have been a good candidate size-wise for a pollinator of *Micropetasos*.

The elaborate appearance of flowers evolved in concert with their pollinators. Petal patterns that are only visible under ultraviolet light may be lost on us but provide useful signposts for the insects that can see this light wavelength. Flowers' scents offer an enticing promise of the nectar on offer—a bribe to the visiting insect, which will be forced to bring its body into contact with the flower's pollen-bearing stamens and pollen-receiving stigmas to get at the prize. While most pollinators are insects, some flowers attract pollinating bats or birds instead, and their evolution has shaped them to appeal strongly to the senses of these animals instead. The use of animals as seed-dispersers is certainly not universal, but many larger angiosperms do produce enticing fruits that animals will eat, and sometime later (and often some distance away) will deposit the undigested seeds in (hopefully) a suitable spot for them to grow, along with a portion of natural fertilizer.

Above *A fossilized angiosperm leaf. The vein system transports metabolic products to and from the photosynthesizing cells.*

Right *Fossils of flowers at Dalle aux Arenaygues in France may date back more than 300 million years.*

Below *Flowering plants make use of insects and other animals to transfer pollen from one flower's anther to another's stigma.*

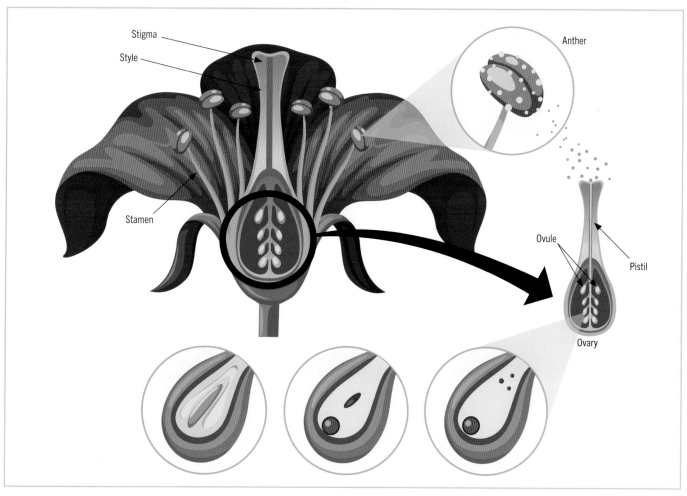

Stigma

Style

Anther

Stamen

Ovule

Pistil

Ovary

The first feathers

The feather is one of the marvels of nature that is as delightful to the engineer as it is to the artist. From head to toe, a bird's covering of feathers offers an all-weather, waterproof garment that can trap warmth and shed it with equal ease, a canvas on which the most dazzling colors and patterns can be displayed, and an incredibly strong but lightweight flight suit, which can be folded tidily away when not in use. That such a structure could have evolved from reptilian scales is almost beyond belief, but the bare, scaly legs of birds remain to show us this ancient affinity.

One of the major surprises thrown up by palaeontological finds over recent decades was the revelation that many non-avian dinosaurs were feather-bearing. Our depictions of such dinosaurs prior to that showed them as scaly or leathery-skinned, with only those directly ancestral to modern birds being thought to possess feathers of any kind. Since the beginning of the 21st century, more and more discoveries of feathers on ever older dinosaur fossils have been made, and it is now thought that feathers could have pre-dated the first split of the dinosaur lineage into the ornithischian and saurischian groups, in the early Triassic. If this is the case, feathers existed perhaps as long as 100 million years before the first true birds evolved. There are also similarities between the keratin protein in bird feathers and that found in the scales of their nearest living relatives, the crocodiles.

The earliest feathers were small, soft, and simple, like the down feathers that you will find close to the skin on a modern bird. The branches or barbs of down feathers do not lock together, and their appearance en masse would be akin to a coating of fluffy fur. The earliest dinosaur feathers did not even have barbs but were simple filaments. They would have provided their wearer with warmth, much as fur does on mammals, and would have allowed for efficient thermoregulation. It is likely that many well-known dinosaurs, including *Tyrannosaurus rex*, would have had feathers of this kind.

Above *The earliest dinosaur feathers probably resembled the warmth-trapping down feathers that we find on modern birds.*

Right *We know today that most theropod dinosaurs were quite well feathered.*

Above Microraptor *had bird-like forelimbs, although they bear large curved claws.*

The existence of larger, more developed feathers has also been confirmed in non-avian dinosaurs. For example, some fossils of *Velociraptor*, the Cretaceous big-clawed theropod made famous by its exaggerated (and unfeathered) appearances in the *Jurassic Park* films, show quill knobs on the forearm bone, indicative of large, sturdy feathers like those used in flight by modern birds. Some fossilized feathered dinosaurs, such as the dainty *Microraptor*, show evidence of long feathers on both forelimbs and hind limbs, providing it with four wings, which may have allowed it to glide short distances.

The first true birds

Many people are incredulous when they first learn that dinosaurs, the most iconic of all extinct animals, are in fact not extinct. It is easy enough to accept that birds evolved *from* theropod dinosaurs, but the nature of evolutionary biology means that they therefore are still dinosaurs, just as human beings are still apes, because we (along with the other modern apes—gibbons, chimps, gorillas, and orang-utans) all evolved from one ancestor, which would be classified as an ape.

It is easy for us today to look at vertebrate animals and say what is and what is not a bird—modern birds are very readily distinguished from their closest living relatives, the crocodiles. However, picking out what distinguished a "true bird" from the various other winged and feathered theropod dinosaurs is a great deal more difficult. The most widely accepted definition is that birds comprise the last common ancestor of all modern birds, along with all species that descended from that ancestor (both living and extinct). By this definition, the best-known "early bird," *Archaeopteryx*, is not a true bird, as it is not considered to be a direct ancestor of modern birds. However, it does share many traits with modern birds, as well as retaining some that we would class as distinctly reptilian. Accordingly, it has long been upheld as a good example of a "transitional form" or "missing link."

Above *The iconic* Archaeopteryx*, with its mixture of "bird traits" and "reptile traits."*

Left *The only living bird species with clawed wings today is the hoatzin, and even it loses those claws in adulthood.*

Archaeopteryx lived some 150 MYA, in what is now central Europe but was at the time a coastal region near the Equator. It was about 20 in (50 cm) long, with broad, longish wings, and (unlike modern birds) had vertebral bones to the tip of its tail and feathers growing either side, like the fronds of a fern. It had teeth, and claws on the wrist joint of its wings.

Although we think of teeth and forelimb claws as non-bird traits, they did exist in early bird lineages as well as in non-birds such as *Archaeopteryx*—indeed, there is a living bird species (the hoatzin) that has clawed wings when it is a juvenile. A major early group of birds, the Enantiornithes, had claws on their well-developed wings and, although some had bills, they also had teeth. However, they lacked long, bony tails, and their proportions, posture, and feathers would have made them very like modern birds in appearance. This group was highly successful in the late Mesozoic and included species that closely resembled various modern bird lineages, such as birds of prey, divers, finches, and waders. Their sister lineage, the Euornithes, was also diverse in the late Mesozoic but, unlike the Enantiornithes, they survived the Cretaceous-Paleogene mass extinction and were the ancestors of all birds living today.

// Cretaceous dinosaur diversity— an overview

Above *Life-sized reconstructed skeletons of animals like* Argentinosaurus *give a very immediate sense of scale when you stand alongside them.*

The Jurassic Era was, as we have seen, a time of great diversification in a wide range of plant and animal lineages. Through the Cretaceous Era, conditions on Earth changed in some ways that created more adversity and a range of new challenges, although the event that closed the era was unprecedented in its (literal) impact. Before that occurred, though, many forms of life on Earth continued generally to thrive, and dinosaurs were no exception.

Although some famous sauropod species and genera died out during the Jurassic, the gigantic titanosaurs had their heyday in the mid-to late Cretaceous. One of these was *Notocolossus*, which lived in what is now Argentina. Only a few parts of its skeleton have been found, but they include a 5.77 ft (1.76 m) humerus (upper "arm" bone)—the longest known for any sauropod. Its feet also indicate that it was

exceptionally heavy, possibly even more so than the huge *Argentinosaurus*, its contemporary and possibly the largest land animal ever to have lived.

The armored dinosaur family Ankylosauridae appeared in the early Cretaceous. These sturdy, quadrupedal plant-eaters were ornithischians, and were fairly closely related to *Stegosaurus*. One of the best known of them lived at the very end of the Cretaceous—*Ankylosaurus* was a little over 19.7 ft (6 m) long when fully grown and probably weighed close to 5.5 US tons (5 tonnes). Its body bore rows of bony plates, it had four horns and a short, robust beak, and its long tail was tipped with a hefty club—the overall picture is of a tank of a dinosaur that could not move fast but was physically well protected against predators. Another group of Cretaceous ornithischians were the hadrosaurs—tall, duck-billed and crested-headed plant-eaters that could walk and run on two or four legs. Their bills, like those of geese today, were well adapted to graze on grass, and they were widespread and successful across the open landscapes of what is now North America.

The theropod dinosaurs were very diverse and abundant through the Cretaceous Period—as we have seen, they included many small bird-like species and also groups that are classed as early true birds, as well as some of the most impressive and fearsome large carnivores ever to walk the Earth.

Below *Like many large plant-eating dinosaurs,* Ankylosaurus *relied on its strength and body armor for self-defense.*

MINIATURIZED GIANTS

The Earth's topography in the Cretaceous Period was rather similar to how it is today. Pangaea was by now a distant memory and, as well as well-separated continents, numerous islands formed. One of the biological phenomena associated with island animals is the tendency for large species that find themselves living on an island, isolated from others of their kind, to become smaller over successive generations. This "island dwarfism" can be seen in modern animals such as the Sumatran tiger and Cozumel raccoon, which are significantly smaller than their mainland counterparts. In Cretaceous times, dwarf forms of sauropods also evolved on some islands, such as the Madagascan *Rapetosaurus*, which, at 49.2 ft (15 m) long, was very petite compared to its titanosaur cousins.

// Dinosaurs—*Tyrannosaurus rex* and other giant carnivores

The best known and most celebrated of all dinosaurs, *Tyrannosaurus rex* carries a name to live up to, and this "Terrible Lizard King" has been brought to fearsome life many times in word and image. The largest of its genus, *T. rex* could grow to up to 40.7 ft (12.4 m) long and weigh some 9.8 US tons (8.9 tonnes). It lived in what is now North America and was by some margin the most alpha of all predators in its environment. There were a number of other large carnivorous theropods within the family Tyrannosauridae roaming the world at the tail end of the

Cretaccous Period, and they have left behind some of the most complete and detailed dinosaur fossils ever to be discovered.

Tyrannosaurids were bipedal and had massive, heavy heads with large, sharp teeth, providing incredibly strong bite force, counterbalanced by heavyweight tails that enabled them to run with their bodies held relatively horizontal. Their forelimbs were famously very small, almost comedically so in the case of *Tarbosaurus*—unlike some other theropods, these hunters were adapted to seize prey with their jaws, although

If you met a Tarbosaurus in person, you would probably not take the time to laugh at its diminuitive arms.

the forelimbs may have been used to help hold prey still while biting. They would have hunted other large dinosaurs, and although they may not have been fast runners (given their great size), their biomechanics suggest they were able to walk at a good pace with great endurance. It is likely that they had at least partial feathering.

Of comparable size to *T. rex* was *Giganotosaurus*, which lived in what is now Argentina. Although

similar in appearance and probably also ecology to *T. rex*, *Giganotosaurus* was not related to the tyrannosaurids but instead shared a lineage with the much earlier *Allosaurus*. It was related to the almost-as-large *Carcharodontosaurus*, which occurred in Africa. Another South American genus of large predatory theropods was *Carnotaurus*—the "meat-eating bull," named for the two horns above its eyes, and built for speed. Between them, these giant theropods had an almost global distribution across Cretaceous Earth.

EAGLES OR VULTURES?

Tyrannosaurus rex and its contemporary large theropods may have been huge, powerful, and sharp-toothed, but this does not necessarily equate to them having been mighty predators—some palaeontologists have argued that they would have been more likely to scavenge than to kill. Pointers supporting this in the case of *T. rex* include its extremely well-developed sense of smell, and studies on its leg joints that suggested it was a slow-moving animal—perhaps most comfortable sniffing out carrion at a leisurely pace. Evidence in support of a more predatory nature exists too, though, in the form of healed *T. rex* bites on the skeletons of other dinosaur fossils, including one hadrosaur with a bite injury to its tail, and another that had an actual *T. rex* tooth embedded in a healed vertebra. These individuals had escaped with their lives, but surely many others did not. The consensus today is that the tyrannosaurids and similar-sized theropods were indeed hunters, but probably just as willing to scavenge if the opportunity arose.

// Dinosaurs—Triceratops and other horn-bearers

The dinosaur group Ceratopsia was well represented in the Cretaceous Period, particularly in North America. This group of large ornithischians included the genus that is surely second only to *Tyrannosaurus* in its iconic status—*Triceratops*. With its powerful, stocky frame, upswept bony head "frill," and large triple horns—one above each eye and a third on the snout, this distinctive dinosaur and its close relatives call to mind a rhino, and an adult would have been a formidable adversary against even the biggest and most fearsome of tyrannosaurids in the open North American landscapes where both occurred at the end of the Cretaceous Period.

Ceratopsians evolved from bipedal (and much smaller) ancestors, but over time many lineages became large, powerful quadrupeds. Many had head frills and variably sized horns, and they also had hard-tipped, bony "lips" forming a tough beak, good for biting into tough vegetation. Behind the beak were rows of numerous tough, grinding teeth, which would be replaced continually as they wore down. The function of the head ornamentations is not known for certain, but they may have been used in defense against predators or in territorial conflicts, or as a way of signaling to others of its species. *Triceratops* itself, at 29.5 ft (9 m) long and weighing as much as 9.9 US tons (9 tonnes) when fully grown, would have had little to fear from most predators at the time.

We might expect the ceratopsians to be herding animals, like the large herbivorous mammals that live on open grassland habitats today. However, most fossils of the group are of lone individuals, although some have been found in small groups. The discovery of large numbers of fossils of *Centrosaurus* and *Styracosaurus*, two large ceratopsian species, in the large Alberta bone bed known as Dinosaur Park Formation, may indicate that these two species lived in herds, but could also represent a chance gathering at a

Above *The remarkable "crown of horns" sported by* Kosmoceratops.

waterhole. Other ceratopsian remains have been found at this site, including bones of the striking *Pentaceratops*, a five-horned species with an extremely long, horn-edged neck frill. The most elaborate ornamentations of any ceratopsian belonged to *Kosmoceratops*, a 14.8 ft (4.5 m) species whose head and neck frill bore 15 sizeable horns and spikes.

One unusual member of Ceratopsia was *Koreaceratops*, found (as its name implies) in Korea. This species lived earlier in the Cretaceous than *Triceratops* and was considerably smaller and smaller-headed, with short horns and a small neck frill. Its notable trait was a row of tall upright spines along the top of its tail, which could have represented a form of fin, allowing the dinosaur to swim efficiently.

Opposite *Like many modern-day browsing mammals,* Triceratops *was probably quite comfortable standing up on its hind legs to reach higher branches.*

// Dinosaurs—an array of theropods

The tyrannosaurids are the most notorious of late Mesozoic theropods, with the first birds and bird-like theropods also increasingly well known. The Cretaceous Era saw the rise of many other theropod groups as well, as these diverse two-footed dinosaurs evolved their way into every ecological niche imaginable.

The genus *Spinosaurus*, found in what is now Africa in the late Cretaceous, was a predator whose body was long enough from nose to tail-tip to rival the tyrannosaurids, though it was very different in appearance. It had a relatively long neck and a small but long-snouted, rather crocodile-like head, and most strikingly had a tall sail on its back, supported by bony spines. Its forelimbs were large with powerful claws. It is thought to have preyed on fish as well as other animals, as its crocodile-like jaws would suggest.

The group Oviraptorosauria belongs to the same lineage that gave rise to modern birds. These slender, long-limbed dinosaurs were mostly 6.6 ft (2 m) long or smaller, and had short, beaked and crested heads. They were probably omnivorous rather than predatory like most theropods, but are best known for their nest-building behavior. Some fossil specimens have been found with clutches of eggs, indicating that they incubated their eggs with their body heat, as modern birds do. An earlier bird-like theropod group was the family Scansoriopterygidae, which appeared to have used their clawed wings to climb and glide between trees.

Left Therazinosaurus *had a sauropod-like head and neck, revealing its plant-based diet.*

The genus *Struthiomimus* is named for its resemblance to modern ostriches (genus name *Struthio*). It was a tall theropod with a small head and long neck, a short but deep-based body, and a short, toothless beak, suggestive of a diet that was at least partly plant-based. It had very long hind legs and would have been a fast runner, possibly able to race along at speeds approaching 50 mph (80 km/h); it is also likely to have used its long-fingered hands to hook onto branches and pull them into reach.

One of the largest Cretaceous theropods, and yet not as fierce as most, was *Therizinosaurus*. This 32.8 ft (10 m)-long, upright and well-feathered dinosaur had a long neck and small head, and rather short and stocky hind legs supporting its hefty body. It was a plant-eater, using its height and long, hooked claws to reach into the treetops. It was one of a group known collectively as therizinosaurs, unusual herbivorous theropods that may have competed with the sauropods, and probably relied mainly on their size (and perhaps also those impressive claws) to discourage predators.

Left *A sail on its back, a spiky head ridge and some seriously sizeable teeth made* Spinosaurus *a distinctive and impressive Cretaceous predator.*

// Dinosaurs—the challenge of reconstruction

When a complete or almost-complete dinosaur fossil is found, we can make a fair guess at what the living animal may have looked like. The task is certainly easier than reconstructing some of the bizarre invertebrate fossils from Cambrian-Era rocks. It helps considerably that we have at our disposal a wide variety of extant vertebrate animals, which are not so different to Mesozoic vertebrates, and we can study their bodies to see how skin and muscle fits to bones. This enables us to work out how to flesh out the bones that we have found. However, fossils are rarely complete, and those that are can often be badly broken up, preserving the poor animal in a tortured posture that bears no resemblance to how it looked in life.

Consequently, mistakes have been made over the centuries by palaeontologists in their attempts to reconstruct dinosaurs and other fossil vertebrates, and we continue to learn more about how they may really have looked. An early reconstruction of the extremely long-necked plesiosaur *Elasmosaurus* placed its skull at the tip of its tail, for example. The posture of *Tyrannosaurus* was correctly recognized to be bipedal (those miniature forearms were clearly not up to bearing the giant's weight!), but early interpretations showed it as walking with a very upright stance and using its wide, heavy tail as an additional support, giving it a "tripod" posture. However, biomechanically, this would not have allowed it to move easily at all, and later models adjust it to a more horizontal walking posture, with the tail held up and serving as a counterbalance to the heavy head. Dinosaurs known only from a few disarticulated bones can usually be reconstructed by comparing the bones that we do have to related species with more complete fossil remains.

Body shape is only part of the story—fossils also give us clues about what a dinosaur weighed, how it may have moved, what kind of terrain it inhabited, what color it may have been, and how its senses allowed it to experience its world. A skull reveals the size of its owner's eyes, and of certain brain regions, such as the olfactory bulb, which is associated with sense of smell. The length and thickness of limb bones show how much weight they must have supported, and foot anatomy can reveal whether the animal was accustomed to moving on firm or soggy ground. The type of habitat the animal occupied may give us clues as to its coloration—dark or dappled patterns are common in forest-dwellers, while animals of open country tend to be plainer and paler. Ornamentations with no clear function, such as the neck frills of the ceratopsian dinosaurs, are often interpreted as having a function in courtship and territorial display, and this leads to some palaeontologists believing that these body parts may have exhibited bright colors or bold patterns.

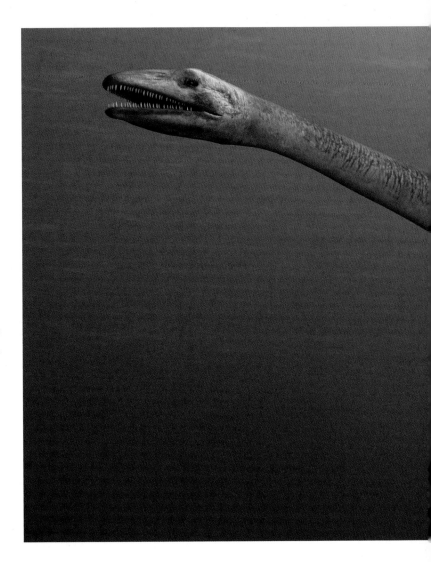

PICTURING THE PAST

Early birds and other feathered dinosaurs are often illustrated as fabulously colorful. However, some artists draw Mesozoic feathered theropods with similar patterns and colors to living species. Is there any way of knowing for certain what colors some of these feathers may really have shown? It turns out that there is—examination of the microstructure of an *Archaeopteryx* wing feather show that it contained abundant cell organelles called melanosomes, which would have given black coloration. The microstructure of the feather also suggests it had a glossy iridescence.

อายุ: ยุคครีเทเชียสตอนต้น ประมาณ 130 ล้านปี
ชุดหิน: พบในหมวดหินเสาขัว กลุ่มหินโคราช
งานที่พบ: ขอนแก่น กาฬสินธุ์ สกลนคร อุดรธานี และหนองบัวลำภู

Phuwiangosarus sirindhornae
Age: Early Cretaceous (130 Myr)
Rock Unit: Sao Khua Formation, Khorat Group
Locality: Khon Kaen, Kalasin, Sakon Nakhon, Udon Thani and Nong Bua Lumphu Provinces

Below Elasomsaurus *as it really looked in life, complete with an improbably elongated neck.*

Above *Thanks to our knowledge of comparative anatomy, we can infer a lot about how a dinosaur was built from just one bone.*

// Dinosaurs—behaviour

Above *Its name means "egg-snatcher" but the eggs found in association with* Oviraptor *fossils actually were their own.*

Over the last couple of decades, clever humans have used CGI technology to reimagine life on prehistoric Earth. Television programs such as *Walking with Dinosaurs*, along with various feature films (most famously the *Jurassic Park* and *Jurassic World* series) bring dinosaurs back to life in a startlingly visceral manner. The way they behave may be tweaked for dramatic effect, but these programs help bring home to us that dinosaurs were highly active in their environments and would have exhibited as interesting an array of behaviors as any living vertebrate today.

One of the most important determinants of how an animal behaves is its diet—another is whether or not it is likely to find itself being part of another animal's diet. Plant-eating dinosaurs did not need to stalk and outwit their dinner, but this does not necessarily mean they were slow and dull-witted, as all but the largest or most well-armored species would have been hunted by carnivores. To avoid predation, some plant-eaters had acute senses, were highly vigilant, and could move at high speed—many also lived in herds, where the vigilance of others would have helped protect every individual. The issue of competition with other plant-eaters led to specialized feeding techniques in some herbivores, such as the therizinosaurs, which used their forelimbs to pull high branches into reach.

Predatory dinosaurs would have employed a range of hunting techniques. The tyrannosaurs were probably not the fastest movers but had great endurance, so could have pursued slower-moving prey to exhaustion. The discovery of birds and flying dinosaurs in stomachs of the non-flying theropod *Sinocalliopteryx* suggest that this predator was a stealthy, cat-like killer, using cover and then a dramatic turn of speed to ambush-hunt prey that would be able to fly to safety if given any warning. Some other dinosaurs were diggers, such as the alvarezsaurs, small theropods that are thought to have dug into termite nests and through broken tree bark to find insect prey.

There is evidence that some dinosaurs incubated their eggs in a nest, most notably the fossil theropod *Citipati osmolskae* individual known as "Big Mama," which was discovered actually crouched on a clutch of eggs—killed by a sandstorm or mudslide, it paid the ultimate price for refusing to leave its nest. Some other larger species may have buried their eggs in warm earth instead, as a few modern bird species do, but may still have guarded the nest site. Young dinosaurs were well developed at hatching age but may nevertheless have depended on their parents for safety and perhaps to bring them food. Discoveries of multiple individuals of different ages that all died together suggest that prolonged parental care occurred in some dinosaur species.

Below *Fossilized eggs of a hadrosaur.*

// New insect groups emerge

By the Cretaceous Period, most of the insect orders that are still with us today had evolved. However, the Cretaceous saw the emergence of several significant and ecologically important new lineages from within those orders. The evolution of flowering plants and their subsequent association with insects led to both flowers and nectar-feeding insects radiating into a wide variety of different forms.

The first true bees appeared in the Cretaceous. Unlike butterflies and true flies, bees are equipped with biting jaws as well as a sucking tongue, having evolved from predatory ancestors. The most likely candidates for the bee precursors were very small wasp-like insects that hunted even tinier thrips. The thrips fed on flower pollen, and it is theorized that the ancestors of bees also began to feed on the protein-rich pollen grains. Pollen is still an important part of modern bees' diets, in addition to nectar. Most bees are solitary but social, hive-nesting bees also evolved in the Cretaceous Period.

Above *Bees have evolved to spread pollen, but also to feed on it.*

Ants were another lineage of the order Hymenoptera that first emerged in the Cretaceous Period. These insects are incredibly abundant on our planet today. Individual ant nests can contain hundreds of thousands of individual worker ants along with multiple queens, and in some species several nests occur in close proximity, causing cross-over of populations and forming a "supercolony" that can cover thousands of square kilometers and hold many billions of individual ants. The impact of ants on ecosystems is far-reaching—they consume vast amounts of organic matter (dead and living) but also support many other species, such as the aphids that they 'farm," protecting them from predators and collecting the honeydew they secrete, and the many bird species that follow ant "columns" to feed on the insects that the marching ants disturb.

Below *Termite mounds are home to vast communities of these tiny insects.*

Termites are the only insect group outside of Hymenoptera to display eusociality (forming a colony with one or a few breeding females and numerous non-breeding "workers" that often have different "jobs"). Like the social bees, wasps, and ants, they also appeared in the Cretaceous—indeed, they were probably the first of the groups to evolve eusocial behavior. Termites and their substantial earth-built nests are a key part of many landscapes today. Many modern animals are specialist termite-eaters, and many more use termite nests for shelter and breeding accommodation, and

fossil evidence suggests that there were similarly specialized dinosaurs and other animals living in close association with termites in Cretaceous times.

Other insects that first appeared in the Cretaceous include the katydids or bush crickets, and the aphids, both of which are important miniature herbivores. They belong to the orders Orthoptera and Hemiptera respectively, two orders of "primitive" insects (which lack a pupa stage). Both evolved well before the Mesozoic but diversified rapidly late in the era and continued to do so after the Cretaceous-Paleogene mass extinction.

Marine reptile diversity in the late Mesozoic

As we have seen, the Triassic and Jurassic saw the rise of giant marine reptiles (and the fall, in the case of the ichthyosaurs). In the Cretaceous Period, a variety of plesiosaurs were still living in the Earth's seas (though the short-necked forms, or pliosaurs, did not survive until the end of the period), and various other marine reptile groups lived alongside them.

The mosasaurs had traits in common with pliosaurs and ichthyosaurs. These beautifully adapted swimming reptiles ranged in size from 3.3–65.6 ft (1–20 m) and had streamlined bodies with forelimbs and hind limbs modified into short, strong, webbed flippers, and a shark-like fin at the tips of their long tails. They were more or less neckless, with strong jaws, and melanin pigments found in their scales suggested that they had shark-like coloration too, with a darker upper side and paler underside (this counter-shading, working against how natural light illuminates the upper side and shadows the underside, is a common form of simple camouflage in both land and sea animals). They also gave birth to live young, meaning that they never needed to spend time on land. Despite their resemblance to pliosaurs and ichthyosaurs, the mosasaurs had different ancestry, descending from the same lineage that gave rise to snakes and lizards.

Two species of modern crocodiles spend a considerable amount of their time in salt water, and all of the group are semi-aquatic. However, their early lineage gave rise to some species that were more well adapted for marine life.

Above *With their half-fish, half-crocodile anatomy, the mosasaurs rivaled the sharks as superlative undersea hunters.*

The group Thalattosuchia is sometimes known as the "sea crocodiles"—it originated in the early Triassic and some survived into the Cretaceous. One of the latest forms was also the largest—*Machimosaurus rex*, a 32.8 ft (10 m) (orca-sized) predator whose remains were found in modern-day Tunisia. In body shape, it was similar to a modern gharial (a crocodilian with a long, slender snout that specializes in catching fish). However, some other thalattosuchians, such as *Metriorhynchus,* were more fish-like, with flipper-like limbs and a tail fin.

Sea turtles first appear in the fossil record from the late Jurassic, while the first that is considered to be directly ancestral to modern sea turtles lived in the Cretaceous. This was *Desmatochelys*, a 6.6 ft (2 m) animal that lived 120 MYA but is very similar to modern species. Other Cretaceous species include the gigantic *Archelon*, which reached up to 16.4 ft (5 m) in length and weighed more than 2.2 US tons (2,000 kg).

Above *The marine iguana of the Galápagos islands is one of the few modern-day marine reptiles.*

SEA SNAKES

Modern Earth is sadly lacking in marine reptile life compared to the Mesozoic. However, the sea snakes form a diverse and fascinating group, and make up nearly 90 percent of marine reptile species today. These graceful swimmers evolved from land-dwelling snakes, in several separate "return-to-the-water"events, with the oldest lineage evolving no more than 40 MYA. However, there were marine-dwelling snakes before this. One such group was the family Palaeophiidae, which included the 29.5 ft (9 m) *Palaeophis colossaeus* as well as a range of smaller species. These snakes had a wide global distribution, and some did survive the Cretaceous-Paleogene mass extinction. The family died out completely some 33 MYA.

// Pterosaurs

The Mesozoic saw the emergence of many new forms of life. However, with dinosaurs roaming the lands and plesiosaurs the seas, it is the giant reptiles that we think of first when contemplating what our world was like in this era. Certain small theropod dinosaurs, including birds, were to conquer the skies, too, but their first flights were pre-dated by an entirely separate group of reptiles—the pterosaurs.

The first pterosaurs appeared in the late Triassic, and their descendants survived up until the Cretaceous-Paleogene mass extinction. They were archosaurs, but their lineage diverged from this group prior to the evolution of dinosaurs. Although they probably bore simple downy feathers, their wings were formed from membranes (patagia) that stretched between their highly elongated fourth finger and their hind leg, making their wings more bat-like than bird-like. They had small hind limbs and when moving on land they were quadrupedal, supporting themselves on the wrist joint of their wings as well as on their hind feet. Most had long, slender jaws, in some cases toothless and beak-like, and many had large bony head crests. One lineage had long tails, while later forms had extremely short tails. Like birds, they had proportionately small and light bodies, and an efficient breathing system involving a system of air sacs that connected to their lungs. They were also endothermic, able to regulate their body temperatures and keep warm enough to be fully active without reliance on ambient warmth.

Pterosaurs included the largest flying animals ever to have lived. The biggest, such as *Quetzalcoatius*, had wing spans in excess of 29.5 ft (9 m), although others were far smaller, such as the long-tailed, snub-nosed and bat-like *Anurognathus* with its 20 in (50 cm) span. Small pterosaurs like this were probably insectivores, using the agility conveyed by their broad wings to chase fast-moving aerial prey, while others may have hunted tree-dwelling mammals and would have been able to climb quickly among branches

as well as fly. Some species were opportunistic land-hunters while others are thought to have been fish-eaters, picking prey from the water's surface with their jaws in low, swooping flights. Some species were capable of swimming and even plunge-diving. Some members of the family Tapejaridae, which had large crests and stout, short jaws, were at least partially herbivorous, with seeds found in their stomachs.

These reptiles often appear to have bred in large colonies. They laid leathery-shelled eggs from which well-developed young hatched—probably flight-capable within a few days of hatching. Whether the parents cared for them at all is not known but perhaps not, given that very young pterosaur fossils have been found well away from nesting sites. Adult pterosaurs of the larger species were very efficient fliers, with long, narrow, albatross-like wings, capable of covering thousands of miles without landing, and of attaining speeds of up to 75 mph (120 km/h).

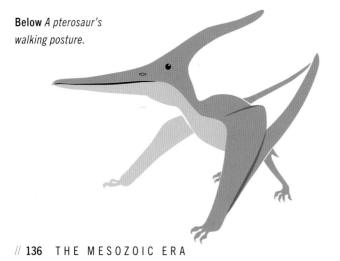

Below *A pterosaur's walking posture.*

Right *Pterosaur skulls reveal the hugeness of the toothless jaws relative to the cranium.*

Below *Artist's impression of a pterosaur in flight—although in truth its long narrow wings would have made for difficult maneuvering in a forested habitat.*

// Other land reptiles

The reptiles we know today are a far cry from their famous and famously huge cousins of the Mesozoic Era. However, alongside dinosaurs and other giants there were also some much more familiar faces—toward the end of the era, snakes and lizards, tortoises and turtles, and crocodiles were also very much a part of Mesozoic Earth's fauna, and they proved to have the staying power that their spectacular relatives lacked. Now, our world is home to about 10,000 described species of non-bird reptiles.

The archosaurs, a group encompassing all dinosaurs (including birds) and also crocodilians and pterosaurs, are considered the sister group to the squamates—the group that encompasses lizards and snakes. The two groups had diverged from their shared common ancestor by the early Triassic, and through the Jurassic, familiar squamate lineages appeared. They included the ancestors of iguanas, chameleons and monitor lizards, and (by the late Jurassic) the first snakes. The 4 in (10 cm) agile climbing lizard

Eichstaettisaurus, which lived in what is now central Europe in the early Cretaceous, is likely to have been an early relative of the geckos.

Snakes evolved from lizards, although there is no certainty about which lizard lineage gave rise to them. Some of the traits that characterize snakes, such as fused, transparent eyelids and lack of external ears, could suggest that they descended from a burrowing lineage, or an aquatic one. The loss of their limbs is perhaps a more obvious feature, but leglessness has also evolved independently in a number of true lizard lineages. Some snakes retain internal traces of hind legs and vestigial pelvises, and some fossil snakes, such as *Najash*, possessed well-developed hind legs and a pelvis, but like all modern snakes *Najash* had no forelimbs at all. This loss, along with the growth of many additional pairs of ribs, is the result of a relatively simple change to a set of

Below *A tuatara, one of the world's best known "living fossils."*

Above *Skinks are a modern-day clade of lizards which, in many cases, have completely lost their limbs and live more like snakes.*

Right *This series of images show a crab which lost a leg and, in its place, regrew a claw instead—an example of Hox genes functioning incorrectly.*

"director" genes known as Hox genes, which control how embryos' limbs and ribs develop.

Mesozoic crocodilians included, as we have seen, some much more aquatic forms than exist today. The first tortoises and turtles appeared in the Triassic, with early forms having teeth (all modern forms are toothless) and an underdeveloped shell and plastron (belly-plate). These were aquatic, with long tails. Turtles' evolutionary relationships have long been debated, but modern taxonomy places them as closer cousins to birds and crocodiles than to lizards and snakes.

TUATARA

To most of us, the tuatara (a 20–24 in/50–60 cm reptile found in New Zealand) looks like any other lizard, albeit a particularly cute and wide-eyed one. However, its skeletal anatomy reveals that it is not a squamate at all but belongs to another lineage that parted ways from Squamata in the early Triassic. This lineage, Rhynchocephalia, was diverse and successful through most of the Mesozoic, with many fossil species described. However, they declined through the Cretaceous—probably due to competition with lizards and ecologically similar mammals. New Zealand separated from the fragmenting Gondwanaland in the late Cretaceous, and took with it very few reptiles and perhaps no mammals at all. It thus provided a safe haven for a single lineage of rhynchocepalid, the ancestors of the tuatara, which then lived almost unchanged to the present day.

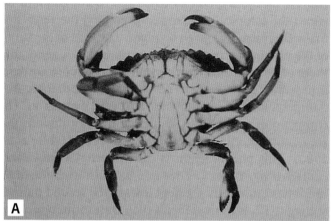

A

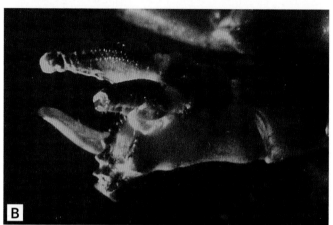

B

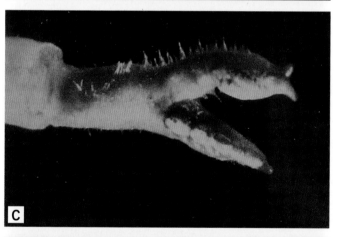

C

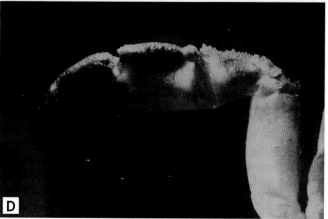

D

// Co-existence of marsupials and eutherian mammals

As we have seen, the first eutherian mammals appear in the fossil record in the Jurassic. Their method of reproduction is strikingly different to the other mammal lineage from which they diverged—the metatherians. Both mammal groups prospered and diversified through the remainder of the Mesozoic Era, although both were also limited by the dominant land vertebrates of the time—the dinosaurs.

Below *Metatherian predators such as quolls are replaced in other parts of the world by a variety of similar-looking eutherians, such as weasels, martens, mongooses and small cats.*

Although the two lineages had diverged, their evolutionary patterns showed many examples of convergence, as they became better adapted to occupy certain similar ecological niches. Convergent evolution explains why sharks, ichthyosaurs, and dolphins all independently evolved such similar body shapes. However, convergence can lead to intense competition, which can in turn apply selective pressure for the lineages to diverge again, into narrower or less closely similar niches.

This may explain the similarities and differences between two of the biggest mammals that lived in the Cretaceous. These cat-sized animals were both native to North America,

Above *Large mammalian herbivores from metatherian (kangaroo) and eutherian (cattle) lineages.*

and their fossils show that their body shapes were rather alike—both were stocky with relatively short legs, a large head, and a massive jaw with a very powerful bite. However, *Didelphodon*, a metatherian, had the sharp teeth of a predator, while *Schowalteria*, a eutherian, had stout grinding teeth, indicating that it was a plant-eater, adapted to deal with particularly tough vegetation.

Metatherians and eutherians co-existed through many millions of years, always in the shadow of the dinosaurs, until the Cretaceous-Paleogene mass extinction, which eradicated larger land vertebrates, including all non-avian dinosaurs. After this event, mammal diversity increased dramatically. True marsupials arose within the metatherian lineage and true placental mammals within the eutherian lineage.

MODERN MARSUPIALS

Metatherians and eutherians co-existed over much of Earth in the late Mesozoic and early Cenozoic Eras, but today metatherians are only found in a few places—most famously, Australia. Few eutherians were present on Australia as it became increasingly isolated from other land masses, giving the metatherian population free rein to diversify and radiate into many different forms. Today, Australia has more than 100 different marsupial species. It is striking, though, how closely similar many of them are, in morphology, ecology, or both, to placental mammals elsewhere in the world. The large kangaroos occupy the same niches as large grazing hoofed mammals, while the many small possum species are rodent-like or shrew-like. Quolls and dunnarts occupy similar niches to weasels, mongooses, and other small carnivores, and koalas resemble sloths in their arboreal habits, leafy diet, slow metabolism, slow movement, and slow-wittedness.

// Birds of the late Cretaceous

As the Mesozoic neared its end, many bird lineages that are still extant today had made their first appearances on Earth. True birds were also more clearly distinct from the many feathered (and some flying) non-avian theropod dinosaurs living at the time, such as the numerous superficially very bird-like dromaeosaurids. True birds had evolved certain traits (particularly in their bony anatomy) that differentiated them from their non-avian cousins, and these traits continued to be modified through evolution, shaping birds into the creatures we know today.

While bird-like wings evolved well before the emergence of true birds, the changes to tail anatomy came later. As we have seen, *Archaeopteryx*, a borderline bird by most classifications, is not bird-like by this measure. Its tail is like that of a modern lizard, with separate vertebrae extending to the tip, and feathers attached either side of this column of skin-and-muscle-covered bone. In modern birds, though, the tail vertebrae are greatly reduced in size and also fused together, into a little structure called the pygostyle, from which the tail feathers grow out in a fan formation.

Another skeletal development was that of a large, narrow keel on the sternum or breastbone. This provides an attachment point for the massive pectoral muscles that power the flapping of modern birds' wings—the musculature in the wing itself is fairly miniscule by comparison. Some flightless birds have lost this keel, but it is a feature of all modern flying birds.

A few bird species of the late Cretaceous can be assigned to an existing bird lineage—though not always with full confidence. For example, *Polarornis*, a sharp-billed, diving fish-eater known from Antarctica, 66 MYA, shows clear similarities to the modern order Gaviiformes (the loons or divers). However, some palaeontologists consider it better placed in the duck and goose lineage. The earliest penguins also probably evolved during the Cretaceous, as clear penguin fossils exist from just after the Cretaceous-Paleogene mass extinction. The group that includes modern chickens, pheasants, and other gamebirds also evolved in the Cretaceous, with fossil representatives including *Austiornis* (although this was initially wrongly considered to be a member of the enantiornithine group, which was not ancestral to modern birds).

Below *The shrinking and simplification of the avian tail.*

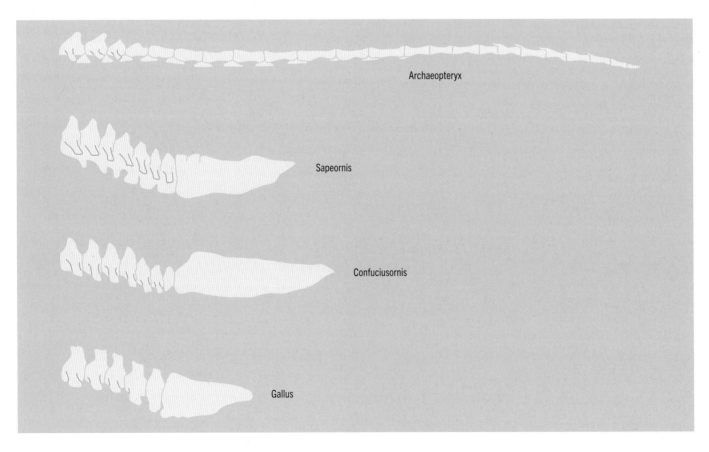

A BONUS BILL

The advantages of flight are very apparent to us (hence our own hurry to develop machines that could carry us through the air). The ability to fly evolved independently at least three times in dinosaurs, as well as in pterosaurs. The flying non-avian dinosaurs, some other avian groups not ancestral to modern birds, and the pterosaurs were all highly successful groups in their time. The extinction of all non-bird flying reptiles in the Cretaceous-Paleogene mass extinction denied us the opportunity to see how these other flying lineages may have evolved over the following 66 million years. The extinction killed off all larger vertebrates, and many true birds were very small, but they were possibly better adapted for survival in other ways as well. One difference that may have been key was the replacement of toothy jaws with a lightweight bill or beak. All weight savings are good news for flight efficiency. The digestive tract adapted accordingly, to carry out food breakdown, and this also helped birds adopt more varied and therefore versatile diets, improving their survivability.

Abb. 87.

Zur späteren Entwicklung der Vögel in der Saurierzeit. Neben dem in Abb. 86 gezeigten Fischvogel lebte am gleichen Niobrarameer der Kreidezeit ein viel größerer Vogel, der königliche Westvogel (Hesperornis regalis), der ebenfalls noch Zähne in den Kiefern trug, aber das Fliegen bei sich offenbar nachträglich schon wieder abgeschafft und sich auf der Fischjagd einem geradezu seehundartigen Leben ergeben hatte.

195

Below *A great northern diver or common loon, modern Arctic cousin to the 66-million-year-old Antarctic genus* Polaornis.

Above *This flightless penguin-like bird,* Hesperornis regalis, *lived in the late Cretaceous.*

// The Cretaceous-Paleogene mass extinction

Many of us feel sorrow that the dinosaurs lived only in the Mesozoic and did not survive into the next era—the Cenozoic, which is our own era. In creative media and serious study alike, we have explored the possibility of recreating them. If only there had not been a mass extinction some 66 MYA, we could have walked with dinosaurs in real life … or perhaps we could not. The evolution of mammals would certainly have taken a very different course had the dinosaurs and other large Mesozoic animals not been wiped out, and the chances are that *Homo sapiens* would simply not exist.

So perhaps we should be grateful that this event occurred, but we may also feel great sympathy with the animals living at the time, which experienced this catastrophe. The event, bringing about the abrupt end of a long spell of very life-friendly conditions on Earth, killed off about 75 percent of all plant and animal species, and was considerably more sudden than previous extinction events. It has left a permanent scar on our planet's geology—rocks of all kinds, all around the

Below *The arrows on this photograph of a Spanish rock formation show the K-Pg boundary.*

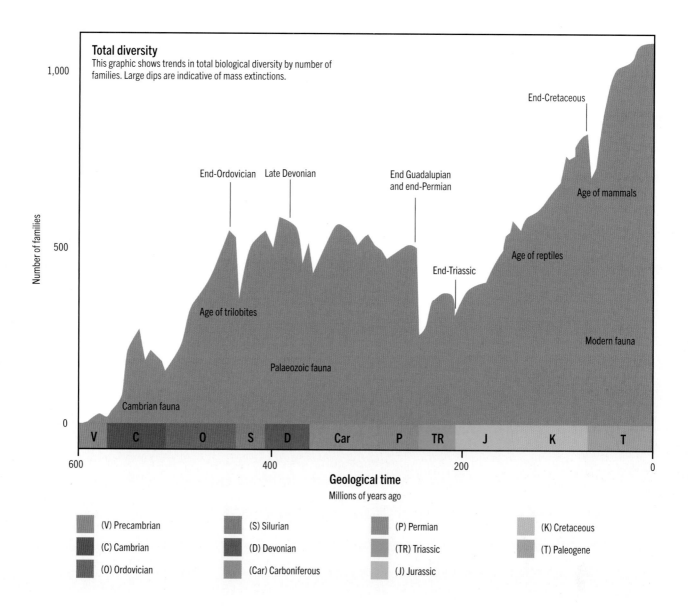

Total diversity
This graphic shows trends in total biological diversity by number of families. Large dips are indicative of mass extinctions.

Number of families

1,000

500

0

End-Ordovician

Late Devonian

Age of trilobites

End Guadalupian and end-Permian

End-Cretaceous

Age of mammals

Age of reptiles

End-Triassic

Palaeozoic fauna

Modern fauna

Cambrian fauna

V   C   O   S   D   Car   P   TR   J   K   T

600   400   200   0

Geological time
Millions of years ago

(V) Precambrian

(C) Cambrian

(O) Ordovician

(S) Silurian

(D) Devonian

(Car) Carboniferous

(P) Permian

(TR) Triassic

(J) Jurassic

(K) Cretaceous

(T) Paleogene

Above *As this graph shows, although mass extinctions drastically reduce biodiversity, the trend is for life to radiate into even more diverse forms following such events.*

world, that date back to that time show a layer of iridium-rich sediment, known as the K-Pg boundary. This can be thought of as a boundary in time, as well as a physical entity—a great many groups of living things, both well known and highly obscure, did not make it across the K-Pg boundary.

In terms of the five major mass extinctions that have occurred in Earth's history, the Cretaceous-Paleogene event was quite average, and not anything like as severe as the Permian-Triassic event. It means a great deal more to us, though, because it affected species so much closer to us, both in terms of our evolutionary relationships and in the Earth's timeline. However, opportunity often flourishes in the wake of disaster, and life on Earth rose to the challenge in grand style.

ARE MASS EXTINCTIONS PREDICTABLE?

It has been theorized that extinction events (defined as any "spike" in the background extinction rate, not just the "Big Five") happen on a regular cycle and can be attributed to some form of natural periodic pattern, either on or in Earth itself, or originating from elsewhere in our Solar System or even our galaxy. However, a close look at the pattern suggests this is not in fact the case, and that life is actually becoming gradually more resistant to extinction events. Since the Triassic-Jurassic extinction event some 200 MYA, Earth's biodiversity has been on a strong upward trajectory, and while the Cretaceous-Paleogene event knocked a dent in this pattern, biodiversity was swift to recover and continue its upward trend. What will occur next, though, with a sixth mass extinction event underway courtesy of human activity, is far from certain.

// What caused it?

The two mass extinctions prior to the loss of non-avian dinosaurs were almost certainly caused by a spate of extensive and violent volcanic activity. A similar cause has been proposed for the Cretaceous-Paleogene event, here mainly involving the Deccan Traps, a volcanic region in modern-day India. Other ideas have included climate and sea level changes, but it is generally now undisputed that the cause was a massive asteroid strike. The asteroid's impact caused the high levels of iridium found in the K-Pg boundary—iridium is scarce on Earth but abundant in asteroids.

Above *The impact that triggered the Cretaceous-Paleogene event would have quickly destroyed virtually all life in the immediate vicinity.*

Asteroid impacts have lessened greatly in frequency over Earth's lifespan—in the Hadean Eon, the number of collisions almost amounted to a bombardment and were one of the reasons this timespan earned its hellish moniker. However, there is always the possibility of another serious strike, and 66 MYA an asteroid thought to be between 6.2–9.3 miles (10–15 km) wide struck what is now part of the Yucatan peninsula in Mexico. The Chicxulub crater now lies partly on land and partly under the sea, but when it struck it would have hit shallow sea. It is 112 miles (180 km) wide and 12.4 miles (20 km) deep.

The immediate aftermath of the strike would have devastated the surrounding landscape—destroying an expanse of seabed and throwing up seawater into mega-tsunamis that would have caused massive damage to nearby land. The accompanying air blast would have been powerful enough to flatten forests in a wide area around the impact zone, and there would also have been a powerful pulse of extreme heat. The impact would have thrown a vast amount of rocky debris into the air, which would have landed as far as 373 miles (600 km) away. The overall effect in physics terms would have been akin to detonating several large nuclear

Above *The location of the Chicxulub crater.*

warheads, and would have instantly destroyed all or virtually all life over a large area of land and sea around the impact site. The first few hours of the Cenozoic Era were devastating indeed, but the long-term and far-reaching consequences would have been a great deal worse.

One of these was "flash acidification," caused by the quantity of sulfur released into the atmosphere by the ejected rock and dust from the impacted ground, as well as the vaporized asteroid itself. This caused acid rainfall that would have affected the seas worldwide. After the initial massive pulse of heat, the Earth's upper atmosphere would also have become choked with fine dust through the weeks after the strike, absorbing the Sun's light and heat and causing a rapid cooling effect. The impact also triggered seismic activity, resulting in volcanic eruptions and earthquakes. This climatic and geological upheaval presented huge survival challenges to those animals and species that had survived the impact itself.

// Survivors and casualties

The loss of the non-avian dinosaurs following the impact of the asteroid made for a complete remodeling of the Earth's ecology. As with the Permian extinction, animal body size appears to have been of crucial importance in terms of survival. Almost no animals larger than 55 lb (25 kg) in body weight made it through the Cretaceous-Paleogene mass extinction—so as well as dinosaurs, the mighty pterosaurs and plesiosaurs were also wiped out.

The effects of acid rain and drastically reduced sunlight had a colossal impact on Earth's plant life, as well as photosynthesizing marine plankton. Prior to the event, the angiosperms were already strongly outcompeting older plant groups, and post-event many angiosperm lineages survived, although gymnosperms fared better. Many of the angiosperm groups that disappeared were insect-pollinated—insects too suffered very heavy losses. In the seas, the ammonites were wiped out, and with them went the ammonite-eating mosasaurs.

Mammal extinctions included the loss of almost all metatherians from North America, setting the stage for a complete takeover by eutherian mammals here as the Cenozoic Era progressed. While true bird lineages survived, the extremely bird-like (and classed as birds by some authorities) Enantiornithes were wiped out. Fishes in marine and fresh waters had varied fortunes—those living in the deepest oceans were spared from the worst, but many other families that specialized in shallower open and seabed habitats died out, with the skates and rays especially hard-hit.

Above *An ability to lie dormant for long periods helped the crocodilians to beat the odds and be among the tiny number of larger animals to survive the extinction event.*

Above *The extinction created favorable conditions for many fungi to thrive.*

Although the event created opportunities for evolutionary radiation, these were often a long time coming, and sheer survivability was of greater importance. Crocodilians may have survived through a combination of their burrowing habits and ability to survive long spells without food (nevertheless, all large species did die out). Small but strongly flying birds, with their modest food requirements and high mobility, were better placed to survive than larger and slower species, and similar factors favored the survival of small mammals.

MUSHROOMING SUCCESS

Certain groups of saprophytic fungi were perhaps the most fortunate of all organisms, possessing an array of traits that set them up well to not only survive but also thrive in the apocalyptic landscapes of the very early Cenozoic. As non-photosynthesizers, they did not require sunlight to live, but instead were ecological decayers, and dead organic matter would have been present in great abundance. Rocks from this time period show a dramatic increase in fossilized fungal spores, indicating a surge in fungal abundance and diversity. It may have seemed for a time that the Cenozoic would be the Age of Fungi, but this situation was not sustainable, and for life to continue, some photosynthesizers would have had to survive and, in time, recover. Thankfully, enough of them did survive, and the planet healed, so the survivors recovered and, gradually, began to thrive again.

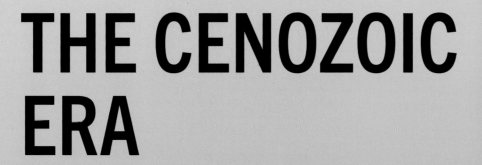

THE CENOZOIC ERA

For millennia, life on Earth was extremely challenging for the survivors of the Cretaceous–Tertiary mass extinction. However, as the dust literally settled, this community of small-bodied animals began their own process of adaptive radiation. Birds, the sole surviving dinosaurs, honored their lost relatives and became the most diverse group of land vertebrates, while modern mammal groups emerged and, eventually, new giants roamed the land and seas. Flowering plants, now the dominant plant life on land, co-evolved with insects, forming associations that shaped the diversification of both into an array of strange and beautiful forms. The Cenozoic also saw the emergence of our own, human lineage.

A recreation of a woolly mammoth. They were about the same height as a modern African elephant, but with much smaller ears, to keep them from losing heat in cold climates.

// Overview of the era

The era that began after the end of the Cretaceous, the last period of the Mesozoic, is known as the Cenozoic Era. At just 66 million years old (compared to 186 million years for the entire duration of the Mesozoic), this is the era that Earth is in at present, and so far, consists of three periods of geological time. These are the Paleogene (from 66 to 23.03 MYA), the Neogene (from 23.03 to 2.58 MYA), and the current period, the Quaternary (from 2.58 MYA to the present day).

These periods are further divided into epochs—in the Paleogene they are the Paleocene (66–56 MYA), the Eocene (56–33.9 MYA), and the Oligocene (33.9–23.03 MYA). The Neogene is divided into the Miocene and Pliocene epochs (23.03–5.333 MYA and 5.333–2.58 MYA respectively), and the Quaternary consists of the Pleistocene epoch (2.58 MYA to 11,700 years ago), and the current epoch, the Holocene, which began 11,700 years ago.

The Cenozoic Era began with the Earth reeling from the shock of the huge asteroid impact that marked the end of the Mesozoic. Through the early Paleogene, the surviving life forms began to increase in number and diversity. With no large plant-eaters, land plants bounced back quite rapidly and terrestrial habitats became forested. The planet became warmer initially, and mammal diversity increased greatly on land, while sharks enjoyed another surge of diversity as they filled niches that had been occupied by now-extinct large reptiles. Global cooling, a general reduction in rainfall, and other climatic fluctuations began in this period and continued through the Neogene. The Paleogene and Neogene also saw further break-up of the land masses that had once formed Pangaea (and, sometimes, some temporary re-joining).

Right *The Cenozoic saw the rise of a new megafauna on Earth, but these giants were woolly rather than feathery.*

Below *The early Paleogene was characterized by extensive forests over much of the land.*

The early Quaternary was characterized by ice ages and droughts, leading to an elevated extinction rate. The Holocene saw the rise of our own species, *Homo sapiens*, and our consequent fast-growing impact on all life on Earth.

HOW DO WE DECIDE WHEN ERAS END?

The division of geological time into eons, eras, periods, and epochs is a handy system for us to keep track of what happened and when, but what is the science behind our allocation of these boundaries? The determinants are significant events affecting the planet and its living elements, as documented through geology. For example, the Permian mass extinction is our marker for the end of the Paleozoic Era and the beginning of the Mesozoic, and the Cretaceous-Paleogene extinction marked the end of the Mesozoic and beginning of the Cenozoic. Significant but less globally dramatic events are used to separate the periods within an era, and more minor events determine the boundaries between epochs.

Placental mammal radiation

As we have seen, at the beginning of the Cenozoic the mammals that survived were all very small in size—their upper weight limit was about 22 lb (10 kg). However, some of these mini-mammals belonged to lineages that were to evolve into much larger forms in due course—among them the whales and horses, as well as our own lineage, the primates. However, the warm climate and forested terrain of the early Cenozoic continued to favor small body sizes in mammals for many more millennia.

The eutherian mammals dominated the planet's northern hemisphere, while metatherians (and the few monotremes) were better represented in the southern hemisphere, but overall both groups had a worldwide distribution initially. However, it was the eutherians that proved more successful over time. True placental mammals evolved through the Paleocene epoch and became highly diverse, although not all of the new lineages that appeared were to survive far into the Cenozoic.

Above *In the order Pholidotamorpha, the modern-day pangolins form the surviving twig of what was once a richly branching evolutionary tree.*

Above *The New Zealand lesser short-tailed bat is an unusual species, capable of walking as well as flying, and descends from a 20-million-year-old lineage.*

Two notable mammalian orders that appeared in the Cenozoic are Pholidotamorpha and Oxyaenidae. These two groups were related, and shared an ancestry with modern carnivores—cats, dogs, bears, and the like. The Oxyaenidae were very carnivore-like in form, resembling civets or hyenas, with strong jaws and rather long bodies with short legs. They preyed on many other vertebrate and invertebrate animals, pursuing prey on the ground and in the trees, and some forms developed oversize "sabre-tooth" canines. Larger forms topped 44 lb (20 kg) in weight. The Pholidotamorpha were a diverse group of mainly ant-eating mammals. Some resembled modern moles, and others were more similar to

anteaters. Oxyaenidae did not survive beyond the Eocene, and nearly all of Pholidotamorpha also died out, but one lineage survived—the pangolins. These peculiar ant-eating mammals, with their pinecone-like skin shields, are widespread today in Africa and Asia (though most species are endangered).

Bats, the only flying mammals and today the second most diverse mammalian group, emerged in the Eocene. A paucity of fossils means that their relationships with other mammal groups have long been mysterious, but those fossils that have been found, coupled with insights from genetic study, reveal that bats emerged from a group known as Laurasiatheria. This very diverse group, which originated on the continent of Laurasia, includes carnivores, hoofed mammals and insectivores, and it is likely that the first precursors to bats were small, gliding, insect-eating species.

// Sharks rule the oceans

Shark abundance and diversity was impressive by the late Mesozoic. Sharks, like most other fish, were hard-hit by the Cretaceous-Paleogene mass extinction, but unlike the great marine reptiles, some survived and inherited a watery world that was much less filled with competitors than before. This triggered another spell of adaptive radiation, and some of the most remarkable sharks ever to swim our seas appeared through the Cenozoic.

The genus *Scapanorhynchus*, related to the peculiar and still-living goblin shark, included several very slim sharks with exaggeratedly long, pointy noses (the name means "spade-snout"), that ranged in size from 26 in–9.84 ft (65 cm–3 m). These sharks lived in the Paleogene and beyond, in deep, dark water and probably found prey by sensing their electrical fields, as the goblin shark does today.

Thresher sharks are notable for their unusual tails, which have a hugely enlarged upper lobe. Modern species are relatively small but the Miocene *Alopias grandis* was a giant of its kind, as large as a great white shark. The genus *Hemipristis* belonged to the group known as weasel sharks

and, although some were large, the special trick of these species was to attack big prey and take bites of flesh, without necessarily killing their victim.

Perhaps the most famous Cenozoic shark was *Otodus megalodon*, which first appeared in the Oligocene. This shark has been assigned to several different genera over time, which is one of the reasons it is usually known simply as "Megalodon." It belongs to the same taxonomic order as many impressive modern-day sharks, including the great white and the plankton-eating whale shark, which is the largest species on Earth. The biggest examples of Megalodon were probably a little larger than the 59 ft (18 m) whale shark, but this was no gentle plankton-eater. Its speed, teet,h and bite force meant that it could kill pretty much any other animal it encountered, including large whales. The genus *Palaeocarcharodon*, which was highly successful in the early Paleogene after the disappearance of large predatory marine reptiles, may have been ancestral to Megalodon, though unlike Megalodon it had serrated teeth.

Opposite *A sudden drop in competition paved the way for an explosion in shark diversity through the Cenozoic, with the impressive* Otodus megalodon *the most notorious.*

Above *Thresher sharks, with their distinctive tail shapes, were represented by some huge species in the Miocene.*

// Forests flourish from pole to pole

A warm climate and a landscape devoid of large herbivores meant that it was boom time for plants in the early Cenozoic, once the Earth's atmosphere had cleared enough dust debris to allow sunlight through unhindered. Soon, dense and warm tropical or subtropical forest covered almost the entire land area of the Earth, as there were no polar ice caps and rainfall was high. Polar plant life did have to be adapted to a very different pattern of light and dark to what occurred in temperate and equatorial regions, though.

Ferns thrived in these forests, but over time were outcompeted by the surviving gymnosperms and, especially, angiosperms. However, insects were still much depleted in number, so insect-pollinated gymnosperms (both herbaceous and woody) were at a disadvantage for the first 9 million years of the Paleogene. The flip side of this, however, was that plant-eating insects were just as scarce as the vertebrate herbivores, at least initially. Although deciduous plants fared somewhat better than evergreens in the Cretaceous-Paleogene extinction event, thanks to their capacity for dormancy, as the Paleogene progressed, the consistent warm temperatures in most areas favored evergreen plants over deciduous ones, as there was no advantage in shedding leaves ahead of a warm winter.

Small mammals and birds thrived in these forests, especially as plant diversity increased, and this in turn meant the structure of the forests became more varied. Many angiosperms that produced fruits became adapted to recruit these animals as seed-dispersers, producing larger and more nutrient-rich fleshy fruits to encourage the animals to consume them and excrete the seeds in different areas. The continents by this point were well separated but there were still some connection points in the form of land bridges, which allowed newly evolved animals and plants alike to move between land masses.

PETM

The increasing temperatures on Earth ended with the Paleocene–Eocene Thermal Maximum (PETM), when large amounts of carbon rapidly entered our atmosphere, and caused global temperatures to spike by 9–14°F (5–8°C). This event, still of unknown cause, marked the end of the Paleocene epoch and the start of the Eocene, and had a significant impact on the composition of plant life on Earth. Many species went extinct, but others, better adapted for a hotter environment, thrived and diversified. Although rapid for an event of this type, the PETM took place at just $1/_{500th}$ of the speed that our planet is currently warming, so should not be taken as evidence that hyperthermal events are not harmful to our planet's ecology.

Right *Antarctic beech trees in Queensland, Australia. This tree's distribution pattern reveals the historical connection between southern-hemisphere continents.*

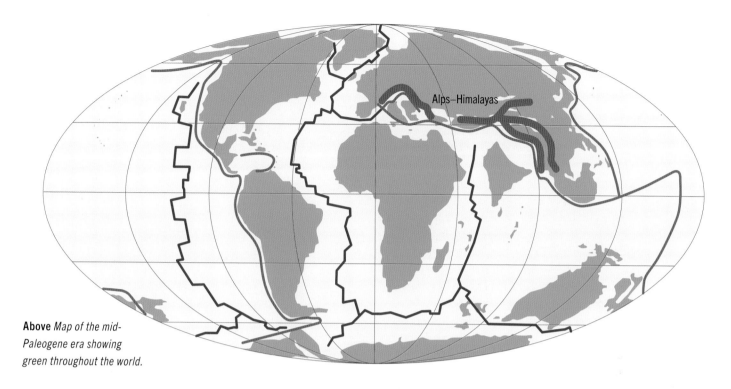

Alps–Himalayas

Above *Map of the mid-Paleogene era showing green throughout the world.*

// The advent of "big birds"

Constraints upon land vertebrate body sizes were no longer a factor after the Cretaceous-Paleogene extinction event, and larger forms began to evolve, including herbivores, meat-eaters, and omnivores. By the mid-Paleogene, some truly tremendous bird species were living on Earth, especially after the PETM when the now-cooling climate allowed open grassy landscapes to replace areas of closed-canopy forest.

One of the early giant birds was *Gastornis*, which appeared in the mid-Paleogene. Its fossils reveal a sturdy, flightless bird with a shortish but massively strong and heavy bill, thought to be adapted for eating tough vegetation. The largest species stood about 6.6 ft (2 m) tall, and the genus as a whole ranged across North America and northern Eurasia.

The family Phorusrhacidae, the "terror birds," emerged in the mid-Paleogene in South America, and were similar in general appearance to *Gastornis*, including sporting a massive heavy-duty bill. However, this bill bore a curve and a hook, and these species were very likely to have been predators. Further evidence of this is the discovery of fossilized pellets (containing regurgitated bones) in close proximity to the fossilized birds themselves. The biggest of them stood some 9.84 ft (3 m) tall and must have cut an imposing figure as it stalked the plains, hunting rodents and hoofed mammals. This family proved great survivors, living into the Quaternary Era.

Giant species of penguins also appeared in the Cenozoic, with some Eocene species standing taller than an average modern human. Fossil remains of very large penguins have been found widely in New Zealand, South America, and Antarctica. Apart from their mighty size, these birds were probably not so different to the penguins we know today, spending much of their lives in the ocean, where they were able to chase down fish with their impressive underwater swimming speed.

THE RETURN OF TEETH

Although the bird lineage had jettisoned true, jaw-rooted teeth, one well-known prehistoric lineage evolved pronounced bony tooth-like structures along the cutting edges of their bills. The Odontoanserae or pseudotooth birds were seabirds that fed on fish and other marine organisms, and in many respects were the ecological successors of the pterosaurs. Among them were some huge species with 19.7 ft (6 m) wingspans, although even larger flying birds were later to evolve.

Left Gastornis giganteus *compared to a 6 ft (1.8 m) tall person.*

Opposite *A phorusrhacid would have been a challenging prey item even for a powerful saber-toothed cat.*

// Snakes and lizards

Those species of snakes and lizards that survived the Cretaceous-Paleogene mass extinction did so thanks to their small, energy-efficient bodies, their capacity to go long spells without food, and their ability to endure harsh conditions through burrowing and becoming inactive for weeks on end. They outlived the dinosaurs but inherited a world where other vertebrate land animals were able to adapt more quickly, and so they were never to attain the dominance that dinosaurs had enjoyed. Nevertheless, they are by far the most successful group of modern reptiles.

Some early Cenozoic snakes and lizards did attain dinosaur-like sizes. The South American species *Titanoboa cerrejonensis*, which appeared in the mid-Paleocene, grew in excess of 39.4 ft (12 m) long, a third longer than today's biggest pythons. Extrapolating from vertebra size, one fossil specimen may have exceeded 45.9 ft (14 m) in length, and could have weighed well over 1.1 US tons (1,000 kg). This powerful constricting snake was one of several sizeable reptiles that thrived in the warm rainforests of this period, and its dentition and other anatomical features suggest it specialized in catching fish and other aquatic animals, including sizeable crocodilians.

The ancestors of the peculiar worm-lizards lived in North America in the Paleocene. The family Rhinenuridae was a widespread and successful group, though it has left behind just a single modern species. These animals were legless and almost-blind lizards (their tiny and skin-covered eyes could sense light and darkness, but nothing more). Their extremely worm-like bodies suited their tunneling lifestyle, but their pointed jaws revealed a mouthful of very un-wormlike sharp teeth.

THE ENIGMATIC CHORISTODERES

The northern hemisphere reptile group Choristodera originated in the mid-Jurassic and got through the Cretaceous-Paleogene mass extinction, surviving on into the Miocene. These were a varied assemblage of animals, some having short necks and long, narrow, crocodile-like snouts, and others being longer-necked and shorter-jawed, with a more lizard-like appearance. They lived in wetland habitats and were predators, some hunting fish and others taking a more generalized diet. Classifying this group has proved highly problematic. They have variously been considered to be lizards, crocodilians, and members of Rhynchocephalia (the lineage that is today represented only by the lizard-like tuatara). The present view is that they are none of the above but diverged from early reptiles well before the archosaur lineage (birds and crocodilians) and lepidosaur lineage (snakes and lizards) had gone their separate ways. They therefore represent a major and distinct reptile group—sadly one that did not survive to our time.

Left *A worm-lizard attacks its human captor, revealing its decidedly unworm-like jaws as well as its fighting spirit.*

Opposite *A fossil choristoderan reptile, which resembled a crocodile in both anatomy and habits.*

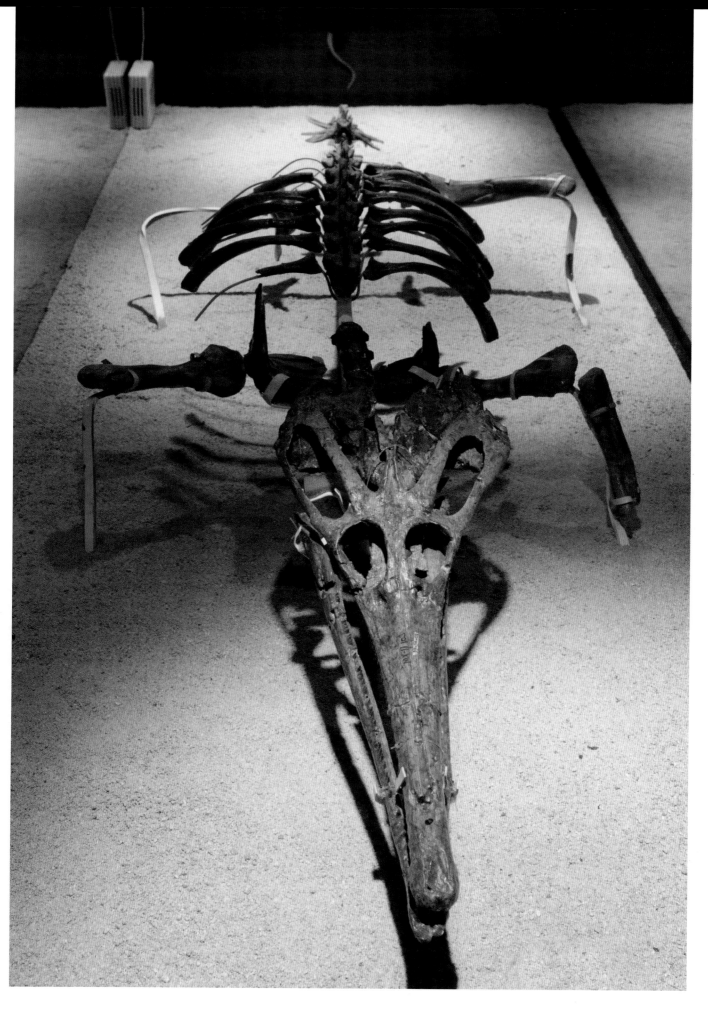

// Crocodilians

Large crocodiles, such as the saltwater crocodile of Australia and the Nile crocodile of Africa, are quite comfortable being entirely inactive for several months at a time. They rest in their burrows and their metabolic processes slow down dramatically. This trait in their prehistoric relatives is one of the reasons why the crocodilians are such great survivors—when conditions become challenging, they can wait it out. Indeed, the crocodiles and sea turtles were the only tetrapod groups in which some species heavier than 55 lb (25 kg) survived the Cretaceous-Paleogene mass extinction.

Nevertheless, many crocodiles did die out, including the well-adapted marine forms such as the huge 16.4 ft (5 m) *Dakosaurus*, with its shark-like tail, possible ability to birth live young, and fondness for preying on other big marine reptiles. Through the early Cenozoic, the surviving crocodilians did not return to such a lifestyle, but increased in diversity nonetheless, with some forms becoming fully adapted to living on land instead.

Several pre-Cenozoic crocodilians were very large, but one of the biggest ever lived in the Miocene. The 32.8–39.4 ft (10–12 m) *Purussaurus*, found in South America, looked and

Above Dakosaurus *was well adapted to permanent aquatic life.*

Above *The gharial is one of just two modern-day surviving gavialid species, both very rare and found only in Asia.*

behaved quite similarly to many large modern crocodiles, hunting large prey using ambushing techniques. In Australasia, the large Cenozoic group Mekosuchinae included the long-legged and short-nosed *Quinkana*, which could run fast on land and chase down prey. *Quinkana* was probably semi-aquatic, going by the locations of its fossils, but its close relative *Trilophosuchus* was probably a true land-dweller. Another of the group, *Mekosuchus inexpectatus*, was also terrestrial and may even have been able to climb trees—in addition it ate molluscs and other shore-line prey, as its habitat on New Caledonia lacked many sizeable ground-dwelling animals for it to hunt.

Crocodilians today are represented by three main lineages—Alligatoridae (alligators and caimans, native to the Americas), Crocodylidae (the true crocodiles, which occur in Africa, Asia, and Australasia) and Gavialidae (the gharial and false gharial, of southern and south-eastern Asia). All three lineages have numerous extinct relatives from many parts of the world, including regions where the presence of crocodilians today would be quite unthinkable to us—the genus *Kentisuchus*, for example, were Eocene members of Gavialidae, and these crocodilians lived in England and France.

// Early primates

The first basal primate-like mammals were present widely across Laurasia some 20 million years prior to the beginning of the Cenozoic. Of larger mammal groups, they are most closely related to Glires, which comprises the rodents and the rabbits and hares, and the tree shrews and colugos or flying lemurs are early offshoots of their lineages.

One candidate for the first true primate is a small tree-dwelling mammal, similar in appearance to modern tree shrews, called *Purgatorius*. This genus lived in North America in the very early Paleogene and had primate-like teeth and ankle anatomy. The more recent *Darwinius masillae*, known

from one beautifully preserved fossil found in Europe and dated to 47 MYA, is widely regarded as the first strepsirrhine primate—the lineage to which modern lemurs, lorises, and their relatives belong. This group diverged from the very similar Adapiformes in the early Cenozoic, and both thrived and diversified for many millions of years, but only Strepsirrhini survived to modern times.

The other major primate lineage is Haplorhini. This group contains the tarsiers—tiny, lemur-like, nocturnal tree-dwellers, with very long tails and incredibly large eyes, and the simians. The simians include all modern monkeys

Platyrrhini nose

Left *The platyrrhine monkeys, found in the Americas, show a distinctly different nose shape to the Old Word catarrhine monkeys.*

Catarrhini nose

and apes, including our own human lineage. Simians and tarsiers parted ways in the early Cenozoic, and about 40 MYA one simian lineage colonized South America, giving rise to the New World monkeys (Platyrrhini—meaning "flat nose" or "wide nose"). The remaining simians are known as Catarrhini—"downward nose."

An early example of Catarrhini was *Apidium*, a forest-dwelling monkey from Africa, which lived in the early Oligocene. These were a fairly small, keen-eyed diurnal monkeys and lived in groups. Males were appreciably bigger than females, with larger and more fearsome canine teeth, suggesting that they competed with each other for control over the group (and access to the females).

LEMUR ISLAND

Only Strepsirrhini reached the island of Madagascar, meaning that the group did not suffer the fate of their cousins on the mainland—outcompeted by monkeys. Instead, Madagascar became a hotbed for Strepsirrhini diversity, and remains so today. Some of the extinct forms of Madagascan lemur included *Archaeoindris*, a member of a group known as sloth lemurs, though in life it would have struck us as more akin to a gorilla than a sloth with its powerful forelimbs, great size (weighing as much as 160 kg/353 lb), and willingness to forage and move on the ground.

Above *A sloth lemur skull from Madagascar.*

Below *Purgatorius, an early Paleogene "proto-primate" despite its distinctly shrew-like or rat-like appearance.*

// Grasses and grazers

After the very warm climatic conditions of the early Cenozoic, things began to cool down in the later years of the Paleogene. This had a dramatic impact on the vegetation of the planet. The composition of the forests in polar regions began to change as more cold-tolerant species prevailed, but eventually no forests could survive in these places at all. Elsewhere, woodlands thinned out, especially in drier regions, and grasses, hardy flowering plants that had evolved in the very late Cretaceous, were able to colonize open spaces and create extensive grassland areas.

Grass is by its nature a difficult foodstuff for animals to consume. Its cells incorporate silica, which is tough to chew and equally tough to digest. Animals that feed on grass are well adapted to this challenging diet, but it has taken many years of evolution for efficient grass-munchers—whether they are insects, birds, or mammals—to appear.

The animals we think of first as grazers are the large hoofed mammals with their complex stomachs—cattle and the like. These animals, the ruminants (named after the rumen—part of the digestive tract in which chewed-up grass is fermented) emerged from the lineage Artiodactyla, which also includes deer, antelopes, and pigs, though not horses, which (along with tapirs and rhinos) form the sister group Perissodactyla. Early artiodactyls, such as the long-tailed, rabbit-sized *Diacodexis* of the early Paleogene, fed on soft leaves. Larger grazing artiodactyls did not emerge until the Miocene. In a surprising twist to the tail, one artiodactyl lineage followed a semi-aquatic and then fully aquatic lifestyle, losing their hooves and much more besides but gaining a whole suite of watery adaptations, and in the millions of years that followed, they evolved into modern-day whales and dolphins.

Below *Over much of the world, the lagomorphs (rabbits and hares) have been outcompeted by hoofed grazers.*

Above *Locusts are among the world's most effective consumers of grasses and other vegetation.*

Left *Grasslands form an important habitat over many parts of the world.*

OTHER GRAZERS

The rabbits and hares, relatives of rodents and known collectively as lagomorphs, were once a very successful group. Although generally outcompeted by artiodactyls and nowhere near as diverse today as they once were, some small forms of these fleet-footed grazers are still very abundant and successful. The grasshoppers, grass-eating relatives of crickets and katydids, evolved in the mid- to late Cenozoic. Geese, one of the few groups of modern grass-eating birds, come from a pre-Cenozoic lineage, with early Cenozoic species including the flightless, 44 lb (20 kg) *Garganornis* from Italy.

// A great many great whales

With the mighty sea reptiles gone and never to return, the sharks became the uncontested alpha predators of the seas as the Cenozoic began. However, by 50 MYA the first true whales had evolved, and this lineage was destined to become one of the most diverse and widespread of all mammal lineages. Over time, some whale species became even larger than the greatest sharks and competed with them successfully as both alpha predators and the most enormous of plankton-eating filter-feeders.

Below *Early cetaceans such as* Ambulocetus *somewhat resembled large versions of modern semi-aquatic mammals, such as otters and water shrews.*

Above *The asymmetrical skull of a beluga.*

Whales, dolphins, and porpoises are collectively known as cetaceans. There are two surviving lineages—Mysticeti (the baleen or great whales, which are filter-feeders, sifting large quantities of small aquatic prey out of water through comb-like baleen or "whalebone" plates in their mouths) and Odontoceti (the toothed whales, dolphins, and porpoises, which have pointed conical teeth and take larger prey). Before these two groups emerged, an array of very different-looking cetaceans swam our seas, but prior to that, the earliest members of the whale lineage were running about on dry land.

Pakicetus, although a member of the hoofed mammal group Artiodactyla, strikes us as wolf-like, with its long and robust limbs, powerful build, and long snout with sharp teeth. It may have ventured into the water to find food but was basically a land-dweller. Members of this genus of the earliest cetaceans lived in southern Asia 50 MYA. From the same region and almost as ancient, *Ambulocetus* was another four-limbed cetacean, but clearly adapted to spending much time in the water—its fossils recall a crocodile rather than a wolf. More recent crocodile-like cetaceans include the family Protocetidae, also from Asia, which existed as recently as 35 MYA, but by this time the entirely aquatic and much more whale-like *Basilosaurus* and its relatives had appeared. These animals were still rather crocodile-like in head shape, and were slimmer than modern whales, but their hind limbs had shrunk to almost nothing, they possessed small tail flukes, and the forelimbs were modified into powerful swimming flippers.

5천 5백만년 전

4천 5백만년 전

4천만년 전

3천 5백만년 전

3,400만년 전

올리그오세
Oligocene

3천만년 전

2천 5백만년 전

2,300만년 전~5300년 전

마이오세
Miocene

2천만년 전

5백년 전

플라이오세
Pliocene

홀로세
Holocene

ECHOLOCATION

The ability to navigate by emitting sounds and analyzing their reflected echoes has evolved several times in the natural world, including twice in the toothed whale lineage. These animals have asymmetrical skulls, with spaces inside holding fatty tissue that conducts and amplifies the sound waves that enter their ears. The lineages of baleen and toothed whales parted ways some 36 MYA and the first fossils of toothed whales with skull asymmetry appeared about 30 MYA. However, basilosaurids also had asymmetrical skulls, and while they are not thought to have echolocated, they appear to have possessed keen directional hearing.

Above *The skeleton of* Ambulocetus, *revealing its streamlined, short-necked form.*

Seals take to the water

The mammal order Carnivora, which mainly prey on other vertebrates, originated in the early Cenozoic, about 60 MYA. This group, part of the larger Laurasiatheria, divided into two main branches, Feliformia ("cat-shaped") and Caniformia ("dog-shaped"). The former group includes cats, hyenas, civets, and genets, while the larger Caniformia includes dogs, weasels, raccoons, and bears. Between them, the members of Carnivora range from very big to very small. They include solitary ambush-hunters, pack and clan animals, climbers, diggers, and runners. A few are strong swimmers too, most notably the otters and the polar bear. One other "dog-shaped" Carnivora lineage, though, is far more specialized than the rest in its adaptation to a watery lifestyle—the seals.

Seals, sealions, and the walrus are collectively known as pinnipeds. They are well adapted to a life spent mostly at sea, pursuing fish and squid underwater with fast swimming powered by limbs modified into flippers. Many species live in cold climates and keep warm with an insulating layer of fat (blubber). Their eyes, ears, and noses are adapted to prolonged submersion. However, they give birth on land, and in some cases the pups need weeks of growth before they can swim.

Below *Evolutionary tree of pinniped lineages.*

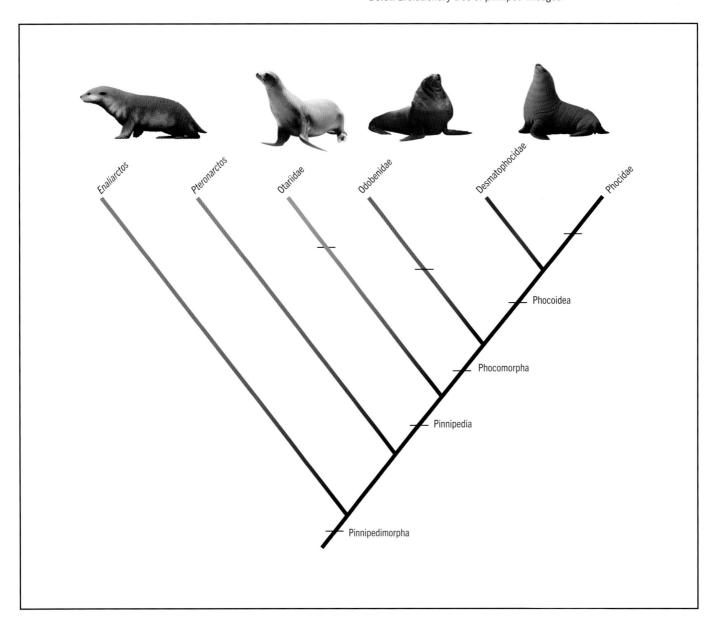

The Arctic, freshwater species *Puijila darwini* was an early member of the seal lineage, living some 23 MYA. It stood upright on four short but sturdy limbs, with long, spreading, webbed toes, resembling a stocky otter. Another genus living at the same time, the sea-going *Enaliarctos*, was much more seal-like, with true flippers, and this genus may be directly ancestral to modern seals. Another pinniped, *Potamotherium*, lived at around the same time, and would have looked rather like the modern giant otter of South America, with a long tail and long neck as well as legs fully capable of walking on land. It was in fact originally classified as a mustelid (the lineage that includes otters, as well as weasels, martens, and badgers). We can see, therefore, that these first pinnipeds radiated into a range of forms to suit land and sea habitats, but it is only the streamlined, flippered forms that survived to modern times.

THE LONELY WALRUS

The most distinctive pinniped is perhaps the large and ponderous (on land, at least) walrus, with its tusked face and crinkly body. It is the only species in its family today, but Odobenidae, which emerged in the middle Miocene, once included more than a dozen other genera. Prehistoric walruses were very widespread through the Miocene and quite diverse in form, some big and some small, some bearing large tusks and others none. *Pontolis* was the largest at 4.4 US tons (4,000 kg) and 13.1 ft (4 m) in length, making it about as large as the biggest living pinniped, the southern elephant seal. Some other early walruses were much smaller, such as *Proneotherium*, which was a slim, tuskless species that looked more similar to a fur seal or sealion than its modern relative.

Below *Just one walrus species survives today, but many more existed through the Miocene.*

// Flowers and animals

The associations between the flowers of angiosperms and the insects that pollinate them became ever more complex through the Cenozoic. These ancient but elaborate relationships provide us with some of the most interesting examples of co-evolution that exist anywhere in the natural world. Some flowers exist today that, because of their unusual structure, can only be pollinated by a single, similarly unusual insect species. Also, sometimes the relationships are somewhat strained, because one party is endeavoring to cheat the system.

Male orchid bees—beautifully iridescent tiny bees native to South America—visit orchids to collect fragrant oils, which they use to attract females. In the process, they pollinate the flower. This appears to be an inextricable connection—without the orchids, the bees cannot complete their breeding cycle, and without the bees, the orchids go unpollinated. However, this group of bees and their oil-collecting behavior evolved about 42 MYA, some 12 million years before the orchids. And a closer watch of the bees' behavior shows that

Below *Hummingbirds are frequent pollinators of a wide variety of plants.*

CARNIVOROUS PLANTS

Plants, like other living things, need a source of nitrogen in order to build proteins. Most can extract it from the soil, but about 800 species today (from many different lineages, but especially those that grow in nutrient-poor environments) trap and consume living insects. Carnivory has evolved at least 12 separate times in plants. Studies have found that, about 70 MYA, a non-carnivorous shared common ancestor of some modern carnivores (including the Venus flytrap, and sundews, which trap prey with sticky hairs) underwent a mutation that gave it an entire second copy of its genome. There were then "spare" genes for building roots and leaves, and in some descendants, these became mutated into new forms, some of which proved functionally useful in new ways. For example, genes for making leaves made leaves in new shapes, some of which worked as traps, while genes for extracting nitrogen from soil via roots became repurposed to extract nitrogen from stuck insects.

they gather smelly oils from other sources, too. This shows that the co-evolution of orchid bee and orchid involved the orchid evolving a trait that allowed it to exploit a pre-existing bee behavior. It also means that the orchid relies on the bee much more than vice versa.

A much more recent example of co-evolution concerns the familiar red poppy. This plant spread from Mediterranean regions to central Europe about 5,000 years ago, and underwent an evolutionary shift, its petals adapting to reflect ultraviolet as well as red light. This adaptation was driven by a different balance of pollinating insects—its regular Mediterranean pollinators (a certain group of beetles that are very sensitive to red light) were scarcer in central Europe. In this region today, the red poppies are now pollinated primarily by bees, which see UV light better than red light.

Some flowers are pollinated by other animals—hummingbirds, sunbirds, and sugarbirds, for example, are all important pollinators. The oldest fossil evidence of a pollinating bird is a specimen of the small, cuckoo-like *Pumiliornis*, from the mid-Eocene. This fossil had pollen grains in its stomach, indicating it visited flowers (although we cannot know whether this was occasional or habitual behavior).

Above *Not all plant and insect relationships are harmonious— some plants, like this sundew, have evolved insect-trapping parts to boost their protein intake.*

Left *It may look red to us, but for pollinating bees the red poppy's petals are eye-catching because they reflect UV light.*

// The evolution of apes

The apes form a distinctive group within the Old World monkeys, or Catarrhini. The few species living today are distinct from the other monkeys in that they have no tails, and have broader, stronger chests and more flexible shoulder joints, as they are adapted for arm-swinging or brachiating as a means of getting around in the trees, rather than running and leaping. The gibbons excel at this, while the great apes (chimps, gorillas, orang-utans, and humans) retain anatomy suitable for moving around in this way (and chimps and orang-utans in particular are still very agile climbers) but are also comfortable moving on the ground.

The earliest known genus of true apes is *Proconsul*, which lived in Africa some 20 MYA. *Ekembo* was a very similar, slightly more recent genus. These species were tailless and lived in forests. Their skeletal structure did not support comfortable arm-swinging so they would have moved more like monkeys, though the largest species were about the size of a modern chimpanzee.

It was somewhere between 20 and 16 MYA when the two modern ape lineages parted ways. Hylobatidae, the gibbons, evolved in southern Asia, while the great ape lineage, Hominidae, had representatives in Africa and

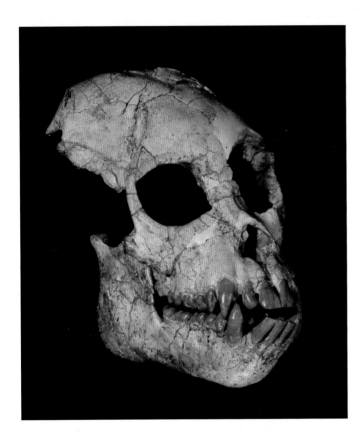

Above *Proconsul, an African species that lived 20 MYA and was one of the world's first modern apes.*

Right *The orang-utans are the only extant great apes to have evolved in Asia.*

Eurasia. Some 12 MYA, one of these Miocene apes was the African *Dryopithecus fontani*. It lived in Europe, in forested areas, and resembled a small, rather light-jawed gorilla. It fed mainly on fruits but possibly also some leaves, and the difference between male and female skulls suggested it lived somewhat socially but with aggressive competition between adult males. This ape, along with other European species, would have struggled when the late Miocene climate became drier and cooler, reducing the extent of forest cover. Today, no ape species occur in Europe (besides humans). In fact, Europe has no wild primates at all nowadays, though Gibraltar has a population of Barbary macaques (nicknamed "Gibraltar apes") which were introduced from north Africa.

BIPEDALISM

All great apes can walk on two feet if necessary, freeing the hands to manipulate objects, but only humans are adapted to do so as a matter of course. The gradual anatomical shifts that made two-footed walking easier included a change in the position of the foramen magnum—the hole in the base of the skull through which the spinal cord exits, and changes in the anatomy of the pelvis and femurs. The African species *Australopithecus afarensis*, well known because of the fossil "Lucy" found in Ethiopia in 1974, is an example of an early bipedal ape, which in many other respects (including brain size and body size) was similar to the modern bonobo. Truly bipedal apes appear in the fossil record some 4 MYA in the human lineage, about 3 MYA after the chimp/bonobo lineage and the human lineage parted ways.

// Mammalian megafauna

When we imagine big prehistoric animals, we may think of dinosaurs first but the idea also summons thoughts of some mighty mammals—mammoths, woolly rhinos, saber-toothed cats. Long after the great dinosaurs of the cooling Cretaceous had departed, some of their ecological niches became occupied by furry rather than feathered creatures, as our Earth cooled down once again through the Quaternary Period.

Above *With its huge domed body,* Glyptodon *recalls some of the large armored dinosaurs of the Cretaceous.*

Only three species of elephants live on Earth today. They are representatives of what was a highly diverse and successful group, including the mammoths and mastodons as well as a wide range of "true" elephants (including miniature island forms as well as colossal species 50 percent larger again than today's largest land mammal, the African bush elephant). The group evolved in Africa but spread worldwide via land bridges that appeared after the Miocene, and those of the far north developed long insulating coats and reduced ears to conserve warmth. The woolly mammoth itself lived through the last ice age, existing from about 300,000 years ago and finally becoming extinct some 10,000 years ago.

The woolly mammoth was one of several iconic species that comprised the "Pleistocene megafauna"—large mammals that lived during the Pleistocene epoch, and eventually dying out in the Quaternary extinction event that began (slowly) some 60,000 years ago and continued until 8,000 years ago. Other northern megafauna included the woolly rhino, the cave lion, the short-faced bears, the Irish elk, the dire wolf, various horses, the almost tortoise-like *Glyptodon,* and various saber-toothed cat species. There were also giant ground-dwelling sloths, large species of antelopes and oxen, and super-sized camels. In addition to the mammals, some very large flying birds such as giant condors also existed at this time.

Above Macrauchenia *was a very large and fast-running camel-like hoofed mammal, which may have been too much of a mouthful even for a saber-toothed cat.*

Pleistocene megafauna also existed in the southern hemisphere. In Australia, there were wombat species tipping the scales at nearly 3.3 US tons (3,000 kg), a 9.8 ft (3 m)-tall kangaroo species, and the marsupial lion, as large as a true lion and the biggest marsupial carnivore ever to have lived. There were even oversized echidnas and platypuses. A cold climate favors large body sizes, as they lose heat less rapidly, and larger prey species drive the evolution of larger predators, with oversized canine teeth for dealing with such big and strongly built prey. However, there was of course still a great abundance of non-gigantic animal species on Earth before and during the Pleistocene, many of which survived the Quaternary extinction event and are still with us today.

KEPT ON ICE

Although fossils exist of various Pleistocene megafauna, there have also been discoveries of almost intact animals, complete with soft tissues, preserved by a natural mummification process as well as by extreme cold. The best known is "Lyuba," a female woolly mammoth aged only about 30 days. She was found in Siberia in 2007 and is estimated to have been preserved 41,800 years ago, after being trapped in riverbed mud. An even better preserved Siberian woolly mammoth specimen was found in 2010—"Yuka" died at about seven years old. Biologists working with her tissues were able to stimulate some cells to show signs of biological function, sparking ideas that cloned mammoths could be created.

Below *The Irish elk stood 6.6 ft (2 m) tall at the shoulder, and had the biggest antlers of any deer species.*

// Continental drift, evolution in isolation

As the Earth moved into the Quaternary Period, the gradual separation of land masses that began so many years ago continued. A map of the time would look very similar to our modern maps at a glance, but there were still numerous small differences, and constant changes through the period. There were times when Asia and North America were connected by land, likewise Great Britain and mainland Europe, times when the Black Sea was cut off from the world ocean and became a vast freshwater lake, constant remodeling of shorelines worldwide the formation of new islands. Inland changes occurred, too, including continued erosion of older mountain ranges and the growth of newer ones (such as the Himalayas, which began to form 50 MYA when the northbound Indian continental plate collided with the rest of Asia, and are still growing today).

By this point in Earth's history, many lineages of highly mobile animals had evolved. Birds, bats and winged insects could fly over land and sea with equal ease; fish, cetaceans and other marine creatures could explore all corners of the world's oceans unhindered ... at least, in theory. In reality, very few animals have this kind of freedom. Their need for a particular habitat and particular set of resources keeps them tied to a relatively limited area, and territorial conflicts can also limit freedom of movement. As biodiversity increases, so does specialization. Natural niches for many organisms become smaller, and isolation of subpopulations becomes more and more likely.

With no gene flow, this isolation can eventually lead to one species becoming two, and it is on small islands in particular that this evolutionary process is most easily observed. Such islands tend to have a limited range of species, which adapt in rather predictable ways, especially if there are no larger predators among those species. For example, many island bird species become flightless, because a lack of predators makes flight an energetically expensive luxury. Also, small species (of birds and mammals alike) tend to become larger, as they have no need to scurry and hide, while large ones

Below *The biogeographical realms of modern-day Earth, each characterized by a particular suite of living organisms.*

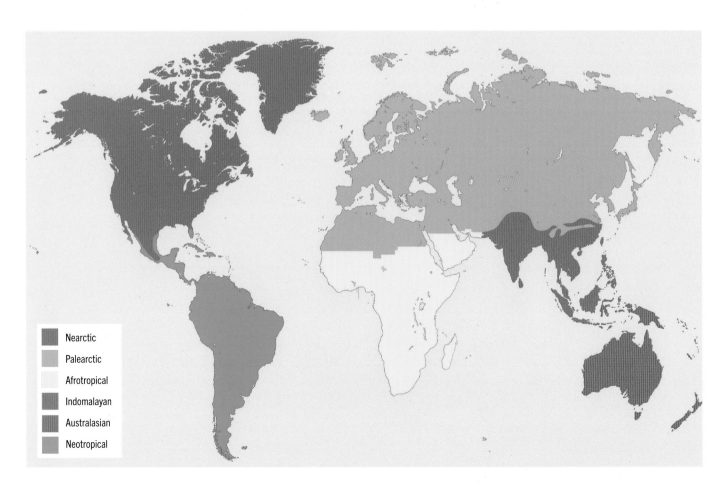

Nearctic
Palearctic
Afrotropical
Indomalayan
Australasian
Neotropical

Above *This partial skeleton of a dwarf elephant species was found on Tilos island in Greece.*

tend to shrink over time, as they are making do with more limited resources in a smaller area. Mediterranean islands such as Crete and Malta, were home to dwarf species of elephants in the Pleistocene, alongside a giant mouse on Crete, a jumbo swan on Malta and various big shrews scattered across the region.

Inland, the formation of mountain ranges can create barriers to gene flow and promote speciation. The same is true of deserts, which also form as an eventual result of tectonic movement. Modern Earth can be divided into eight biogeographic realms, each with its own distinct flora and fauna, and the transitions between these realms are marked primarily by oceans, mountain ranges, and deserts.

Below *The giant otter shrew is one of a small family of mammals found in Africa, and geographically isolated from their closest relatives (the tenrecs of Madagascar).*

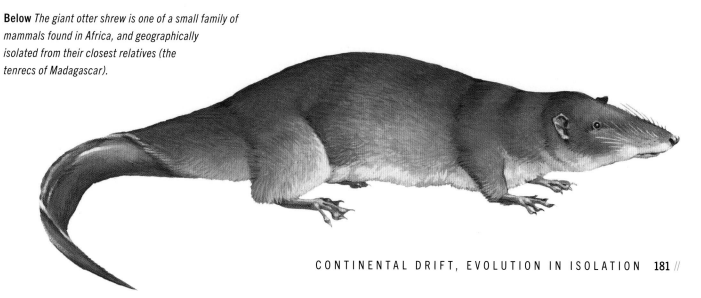

// A cooling planet

Through the Cenozoic, the global temperature of Earth went through a great many ups and downs, and at the present time we are in a "down." The Quaternary Glaciation or Quaternary Ice Age began 2.58 million years ago and is ongoing. Within this event, though, there is a cyclical pattern of warming and cooling, with colder spells known as glacial periods and warmer spells known as interglacial periods. Since the beginning of the Quaternary Glaciation, a full glacial/interglacial cycle has been completed roughly every 100,000 years. The most recent glacial period (which is often referred to as the "last Ice Age" or just the "Ice Age," although this is technically inaccurate) ended some 15,000 years ago, and we are now in the early stages of an interglacial period.

It seems strange to consider that we are currently in a major ice age—one of five that have occurred through

Earth's history and the only one so far to occur in the Cenozoic. However, the periods between ice ages (known as greenhouse periods) are characterized by a complete lack of glaciers and polar ice on the planet, and such a time would feel quite alien to us, and indeed to any of our *Homo sapiens* ancestors—with the first fossils of modern humans dating back some 300,000 years, our species has only ever known ice age times. The last glacial maximum, when the planet's ice sheets were at their most extensive, occurred about 20,000 years ago, after which temperatures increased for about 14,000 years (causing a 427 ft/ 130 m rise in sea levels). For the last 6,000 years, global temperatures have been fairly stable (the most recent century notwithstanding).

The formation of glaciers reshapes the land and coastline, and formation of ice creates overland options for animals to travel. Species tend to shift their distributions (if they can)

Below *This graph shows how atmospheric carbon dioxide levels are low during interglacial periods and rise in "greenhouse" periods.*

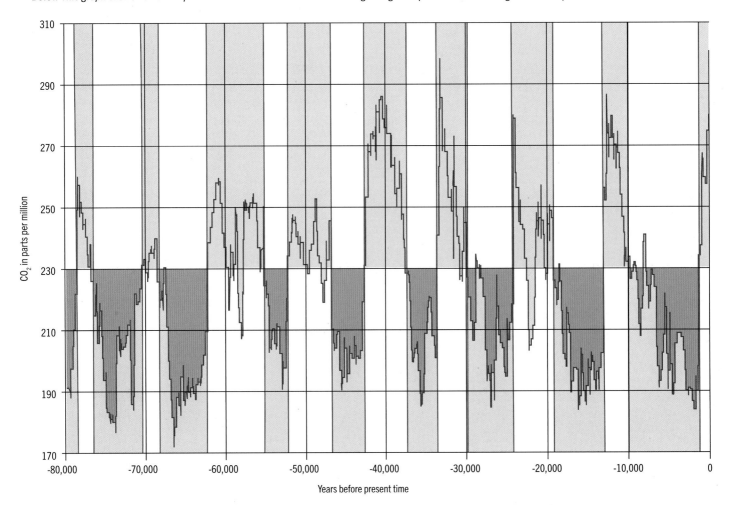

in response to major changes in climate, to stay within the climate zone to which they are best adapted. However, they may not be able to keep up with the pace of change, or they may find that a new environment with a suitable climate is less suitable in other respects—for example, there are other species present with which they cannot compete, or a plant that is crucial to their survival is not present in the new area. Extinctions are therefore likely to be more frequent during transitions between glacial and interglacial periods.

The current interglacial period is likely to continue for another 50,000 years, and then a glacial period will follow, with the next glacial maximum being reached in some 100,000 years' time. Or at least, that would be the projection were it not for the human factor in the equation. The burning of fossil fuels and other human activity is releasing such increased volumes of carbon dioxide into our atmosphere that the glacial cycle is likely to be interrupted.

A valley in the English Lake District, carved out by ancient glacial activity.

// Stasis and change

Change is the fuel that powers evolution. It presents life with two options—"adapt or die." Natural selection only permits the well-adapted individuals to survive and pass on their good traits, and thus steers the population as a whole toward better adaptation, but natural selection is also the deliverer of extinction if not enough of the population measures up. When we look at the living things that share our world today, we can know with certainty that they have, through the history of their lineage, either adapted to change or have not faced significant change at all.

We have a great fascination with the plants and animals we call "living fossils." The term is meant almost literally—we use it for any living species in which a modern individual is extremely similar (at least superficially), to a fossil ancestor or near relative that is many millions of years old. In reality, some appreciable evolutionary change has almost certainly taken place, and that fossil could also have other descendants that have taken a quite different evolutionary path. But there are nevertheless some lineages that have changed a great deal less that most others over the same span of time.

Some environments are more insulated from change than others, and the pace of change is at its slowest in the deepest parts of the ocean in particular. It is therefore unsurprising that some "living fossils" are deep-sea animals. Coelacanths are the best-known examples, but others include the goblin shark and the vampire squid. Further marine animals considered to be "living fossils" include the horseshoe crabs, which appear in the fossil record from 480 MYA, and the lungfish, which come from a Carboniferous lineage. These fish show us that evolution is not the smooth and predictable progression that simplified portrayals would have us believe—we think of lungfish as transitional between gill-breathing fish and lunged amphibians, but lungfishes' breathing anatomy has served them well just as it is, for more than 300 million years. The label "living fossil" in no way implies that a species is not well adapted for survival.

Land-dwelling "living fossils" include the tuatara, which we have met before—it owes its survival to isolation on New Zealand, away from other reptiles that outcompeted its relatives in other parts of the world. Also on New Zealand, the bird family Acanthisittidae (which includes the rifleman, a tiny and particularly beloved native species) is little changed

Above *The distinctive gingko tree had near-identical ancestors in the Jurassic period.*

Opposite *Horseshoe crabs have changed little over their 480-million-year evolutionary history.*

from its Miocene ancestors. However, in other parts of the world where ecological change has been rapid, opportunities plentiful, and competition fierce, other bird lineages within the same order (Passeriformes, or perching birds) have shown dramatic change over relatively short spaces of time. Most famously, Darwin's finches on the Galápagos islands descend from a single species of tanager that colonized the islands only a million years ago, but has since radiated into about 18 distinct species.

LIVING FOSSIL PLANTS

The gymnosperm *Ginkgo biloba* is nearly identical to mid-Jurassic fossils and is the sole survivor of a family that was diverse and widespread through Laurasia in the later Mesozoic. Another once highly successful ancient gymnosperm group, the cycads, still exist in the form of just three families, which barely differ from their fossil relatives. The angiosperm genus *Amborella*, found only on Grande-Terre Island, New Caledonia, is considered the most basal of flowering plants that are still living today.

// The first humans

What is a human? We might reply, "the species *Homo sapiens*," and if we are talking about living species only, that's the right answer. However, all species classified in the genus *Homo* are considered to be humans, and although no others are alive today, many human species have lived on Planet Earth through the very late Neogene Period and the Quaternary Period.

The first human species that we find in the fossil record was *H. habilis*, which appeared in Africa 2.8 MYA. This species walked fully upright, used stone tools, but in brain terms was more or less on a par with modern chimpanzees. More recent members of the genus, such as *H. erectus* and *H. ergaster*, show a dramatic increase in brain volume over a relatively short period of evolutionary time, indicating that these species were under a very high selective pressure to become cleverer. *H. erectus* and *H. ergaster* used fire and created more elaborate tools to prepare their food and to use as weapons for hunting, and they also migrated beyond Africa, spreading from there into Europe and Asia. By 1.3 MYA, these early humans were widespread through Eurasia, adapting to climatic conditions quite different to those they had left behind.

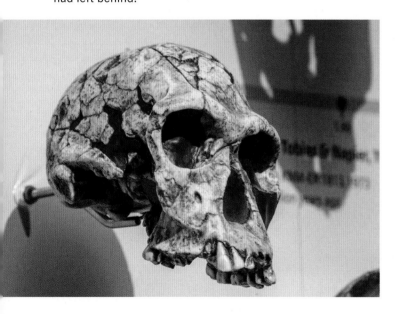

Above Homo habilis *has unmistakably human traits but was yet to grow the big brain of its modern relatives.*

Above right *The face of* Homo neanderthalis, *whose genes live on in us today.*

Opposite *An adult* Homo floresiensis *stood about as tall as a three-year-old modern* Homo sapiens.

However, the earliest *H. sapiens* evolved from other human species that had continued to evolve in Africa, appearing in the fossil record no more than 400,000 years ago. Their descendants also migrated into Eurasia, sometime between 50,000 and 100,000 years ago, and came into contact with the descendants of the earlier pioneers, which had by that time given rise to the species *H. neanderthalensis*—Neanderthals—and also the Denisovans (which were very similar to Neanderthals and may have been a subpopulation of the same species).

H. neanderthalensis and early *H. sapiens* remained very close cousins with many similarities, such as a very large brain size and an elaborate set of cultural practices, including, in all likelihood, the use of spoken language. Neanderthals and Denisovans had more robust teeth and were generally stronger and stockier than *H. sapiens*. These traits, along with a genetic predisposition to store more body fat, were adaptations to cold-climate living and a willingness to eat a very diverse diet.

It was often thought that *H. sapiens* eradicated *H. neanderthalensis* when the two species met. However, the DNA of modern humans of non-African ancestry tells a more intriguing story—up to 4 percent of our modern DNA is Neanderthal in origin (or Denisovan in the case of eastern Asian people). This shows that, in the 40,000 years of their co-existence in Eurasia, the two species habitually interbred.

THE HUMAN HOBBIT

One of the other human species that was still living at the time of *H. sapiens'* spread into Eurasia was *H. floresiensis*. This species lived on the island of Flores in the Lesser Sunda Islands, Indonesia, and is known from an 18,000-year-old skeleton of a 3.3 ft (1 m)-tall female. She was not, however, a child but an adult, and her brain size was much smaller than would be expected for a scaled-down *H. sapiens*. She has now been recognized (though not without controversy) as a representative of a distinct species of human, which evolved in isolation on Flores for many millennia, finally becoming extinct some 50,000 years ago. *H. floresiensis* is also an example of island dwarfism.

// Modern genera

Although a large number of our most familiar plant and animal families already existed by the start of the Cenozoic, many modern genera were yet to emerge within those families. Our own genus, *Homo*, appeared just before the Cenozoic began, making us members of one of the older extant genera on the planet. By contrast, our two favorite companion animals, the domestic dog and domestic cat, both belong to genera born well into the Cenozoic—in fact *Canis* and *Felis* both branched off from their respective family trees less than 7 MYA.

By 5 MYA, many other modern genera had appeared, although they lived for a long time alongside other, often mightier genera. Then the Quaternary extinction event, which occurred primarily around the boundary between the Pleistocene and Holocene Epochs (some 11,700 years ago), killed off a large proportion of the mammalian fauna in many parts of the world. It struck especially hard in Australasia and the Americas, and—as with previous extinction events—disproportionately affected those with a large body size. Large birds were also affected, such as the Asian ostrich, the elephant birds (a group of ostrich-like flightless birds that lived on Madagascar), and the moas of New Zealand. In some areas, many crocodiles and snakes died out. Some of these extinctions were attributable not to natural climatic factors

with the end of the glacial period, but to hunting pressure from a fast-growing population of early humans—although this event also killed off several species of humans.

As with all extinction events, in the wake of loss came opportunity, with evolutionary adaptive radiation ensuring that no ecological niche remained vacant for long. This brought about the emergence of many more modern species from the surviving genera, and life on Earth increasingly came to look like that which we know today.

Opposite *The first feline ancestors of the cheetah and its relatives emerged within the carnivore lineage no more than 7 MYA.*

Below *The difference between the domestic dog and its wild wolf ancestor is testament to the power of selective breeding to modify a genome in a relatively short space of time.*

ARTIFICIAL SPECIES

Every species recognized by science has a two-part scientific name. The first word is the genus to which it belongs (*Homo* in our case—the human genus) and the second denotes its species, distinguishing it from other species in the same genus (so our full scientific name is *Homo sapiens*). We assign a species name to a population of an animal or other organism when we consider that it has become consistently distinct enough, through evolution, from all other populations in that same genus. Subpopulations that are "on the way" to species-level distinctiveness are sometimes given a third name, denoting them as a subspecies—for example, some scientists class Neanderthals as a subspecies of *Homo sapiens* and name them *Homo sapiens neanderthalensis*, rather than classing them as the full species *Homo neanderthalensis*. Some of our domestic animals have become, over far fewer generations than would happen naturally, very distinct from the wild species that we originally domesticated, thanks to selective breeding. We may therefore give these human-made populations their own species or subspecies scientific name—for example, the wild wolf is *Canis lupus*, but the domestic dog is often known as *Canis lupus familiaris*, or even *Canis familiaris*.

Glossary

Biosphere All parts of the Earth that are occupied by living organisms.

Class A taxonomic grouping, in between **phylum** and **order**. For humans, the class is Mammalia—the mammals.

Diapsid A group of reptiles, including modern and extinct species and also all birds.

DNA (Deoxyribonucleic acid) The molecule that holds the genetic code of an organism.

Domain The most fundamental division of life on Earth. The most widely used definition includes three domains—Bacteria, Archaea, and Eukarya.

Epoch A units of geological time into which **periods** are divided. Further subdivisions are sometimes used.

Eon The longest defined unit of geological time. Divided into **eras**.

Era A unit of geological time. Divided into **periods**.

Eukaryote An organism, single-celled or multicellular, with complex cells that contain multiple small structures (organelles). Comprises the domain Eukarya.

Eutherian A group of mammals, most of which produce placentas when pregnant.

Family A taxonomic grouping, in between **order** and **genus**. For humans, the family is Hominidae—the great apes.

Fossil The preserved remains of an organism (or its tracks, droppings, or other traces) from a previous geological time.

Genome The complete set of genetic material carried by an organism.

Genus A taxonomic grouping, in between **family** and **species**. For humans, the genus is *Homo*.

Glacial period An interval of especially low temperatures during an **ice age**.

Ice age A long-term glaciation event on Earth.

Interglacial period An interval of higher temperatures during an **ice age**.

Kingdom In most usages, the highest-level taxonomic grouping, comprising several **phyla**. For humans, the kingdom is Animalia—animals.

Lineage A continuous evolutionary line of ancestry.

Mass extinction A period of time when species die out at a much faster rate than usual.

Metatherian A group of mammals, most of which bear embryonic young that they carry in a pouch.

Natural selection The process by which evolution proceeds, with individuals with the most favorable traits surviving to pass on their "good genes" to the next generation.

Niche An ecological position or "job" that a species can occupy—for example as a tree-dwelling insect-eater, or a plant that attracts bats to pollinate it.

Order A taxonomic grouping, in between **class** and **family**. For humans, the order is Primates.

Organic Describes the molecules that form the cells and tissues of living organisms, formed primarily from carbon, hydrogen, oxygen, and nitrogen.

Ornithischian One of the three main dinosaur groups. A diverse group of mainly herbivores, united by their bird-like hip structure.

Period A unit of geological time. Divided into **epochs**.

Phylum A taxonomic grouping, in between **kingdom** and **class**. For humans, the order is Chordata—animals with a spinal cord.

Prokaryote A simple, single-celled organism, with cells that do not contain multiple small structures (organelles). Includes Bacteria and Archaea.

RNA (Ribonucleic acid) A molecule that can carry and transcribe genetic coding.

Sauropod One of the three main dinosaur groups. Long-necked, often enormous herbivores.

Sexual reproduction Reproducing by combining genetic material from two individuals to create a genetically unique offspring.

Sprawling gait Having the legs splayed out to the sides of the body.

Synapsid A group comprising mammal-like reptiles and mammals.

Tectonic movement The continuous motion of the rocky plates that form the Earth's crust.

Therapsid A group of synapsids, including all modern mammals.

Theropod One of the three main dinosaur groups. Usually bipedal and carnivorous. Includes modern birds.

Trackway A series of footsteps on soft ground, which may be fossilized.

Upright gait Having the legs upright under the body.

Index

abiogenesis 17
alligators 165
ammonites 40–1
amniote eggs 62–3
angiosperms 148, 158
animals
    arrival of 28–9
    Cambrian Explosion 36–7
    on land 46–7
Anning, Mary 103
Anomalocaris 39, 43, 47
ants 132
apes 176–7
aphids 133
Archaeopteryx 7, 119, 129, 142
Archean Eon 10–29
archosaurs 78–9

bats 155
bees 132, 174
behaviour of dinosaurs
    130–1
Bicellum 27, 28
bipedalism 177
birds
    in Cenzoic Era 160–1
    in Cretaceous-Paleogene
    extinction event 149
    in Cretaceous Period
    142–3
    eggs of 62–3
    first true 118–19
    giant 160–1
    in Quaternary extinction
    event 188
Buckland, William 100
Burgess Shale 38–9, 42
bush crickets 133

caimans 165
Cambrian Explosion 36–7,
    52
Cambrian Period 32–3,
    36–7, 112
Carboniferous forests 56–7,
    58–9
Carboniferous Period 32, 55,
    56, 64, 92, 112
Cenzoic Era 152–89
cephalopods 112–13
Ceratopsia 124–5
cetaceans 170–1
chemistry of life 16–17
Chicxulub crater 146
chordates 42–3, 52
Choristodera 162
Citipati osmolska 131

classifying life 24
continental drift 34–5, 64,
    66–7, 68–9, 74, 80–1,
    88–9, 121, 180–1
corals 82–3
Cretaceous-Paleogene extinction
    event 90, 104, 106, 107,
    108, 119, 136, 141, 142,
    143, 144–9
Cretaceous Period 40, 74,
    95, 106–7, 120–1, 122,
    124, 132, 134, 139, 140,
    142–3
crocodiles 134–5, 164–5,
    188
crocodilians 138, 139, 149,
    164–5
cycads 56

Deccan Traps 146
deuterostomes 42–3
Devonian Period 32–3, 40,
    49, 56, 60, 66
Didelphodon 140–1
dinosaurs
    behaviour of 130–1
    Ceratopsia 124–5
    in Cretaceous Period
    120–1
    early meat-eating bipeds
    96
    feathers 116–17
    ornithischians 98–9
    reconstructing 128–9
    sauropods 94–5
    Stegosaurus 98–9
    therapods 126–7
    Tyrannosaurus Rex 122–3
Dippy the dinosaur 95
DNA 18–19

Earth
    formation of 12–13
    oxygenation of 22–3
    pre–life 14–15
echolocation 171
Ediacaran Period 10
eggs 62–3, 83
Elasmobranchii 109
elephants 178
endosymbiosis 24
endothermy 85
Eoarchean Era 10
Eocene Epoch 152, 158
Euglana 26, 27
eukaryotes 10, 24–5, 26, 27, 44
Euornithes 119

eutherian mammals 104–5,
    140–1, 154–5
eutriconodonts 101
extinctions
    between glacial/interglacial
    periods 183
    and continental drift 34,
    68–9, 89
    Cretaceous-Paleogene
    extinction event 144–9
    and Great Oxidation Event 22
    in Jurassic Period 106–7
    in Paleozoic ice age 64
    Permian-Triassic extinction
    event 68–71, 76
    Quaternary extinction event
    188–9
    Triassic-Jurassic extinction
    event 90–1

feathers 116–17
ferns 55
fish 76–7
flowering plants 74, 114–15
forests 56–7, 158–9
fossil hunting 41
fungi 48–9, 149

Gastornis 160
gharials 165
gills 47
Ginkgo biloba 184
glacial periods 182–3
Gondwanaland 66, 80, 89, 89
grazers 168–9
green algae 44
gymnosperms 92–3, 114

Hadean Eon 10, 14, 16
Hallucigenia 38, 39
Holocene epoch 152, 153
Homo Sapiens 153, 186–7

ice ages 64–5, 182
ichthyosaurs 103
Iguanodon 99
insects
    in Carboniferous forests
    58–9
    and Cretaceous-Paleogene
    extinction event 148
    modern groups 110–11,
    132–3
    pollinators 174–5
interglacial periods 182–3
invertebrates 46, 49, 52, 58–9,
    85, 112–13

island dwarfism 121

Jupiter 12
Jurassic Period 74, 94, 95,
    100–1, 106–7, 108, 120
land–based animals
    arrival of 46–7
    and soil formation 50–1
    vertebrate emergence 60–1
land ecosystems 50–1
large land plants 54–5
Laurasia 66, 80, 89
lichen 48–9
life
    Cambrian Explosion 36–7
    chemistry of 16–17
    classification of 24
    first living organisms 20–1
    on land 46–7
    multicellular 26–7
    and RNA 18–19
living fossils 184–5
lizards 138–9, 162–3
Lystrosaurus 67, 70–1, 78, 80

Madagascar 167
mammals
    arrival of 86–7
    and Cretaceous-Paleogene
    extinction event 148
    eggs of 63
    eutherian 104–5, 140–1,
    154–5
    in Jurassic Period 100–1
    megafauna 178–9
    placental 154–5
    and reptiles 101
marine plants 44–5
marine reptiles 82–3, 134–5
Mars 12, 13
marsupials 140–1, 179
megafauna 178–9
megalodon 7, 156
Megalosaurus 100
Mercury 12, 13
Mesoarchean Era 10
Mesoproterozoic Era 10
Mesozoic Era 74–149
metatherians 104
Microraptor 6, 116
Miocene Epoch 152
Morganucodon 86–7
mosasaurs 134
mosses 48–9, 55
multicellular life 26–7

Neogene Period 152

Neoproterozoic Era 10
Neptune 12
nocturnal bottleneck hypothesis 87

octopuses 112–13
Oligocene Epoch 152
Ordovician Period 32, 33, 64
ornithischians 98–9
Otodus megalodon 156
Oviraptor 6
Oxyaenidae 155
oxygen 22–3, 37, 59

Paleoarchean Era 10
Paleocene–Eocene Thermal Maximum (PETM) 158, 160
Paleocene Epoch 152, 158, 162
Paleogene Period 152
Paleoproterozoic Era 10
Paleozoic Era 10, 32–71
Pangea 64, 66–7, 68, 74, 80, 84, 88–9
Permian Period 64, 68–9, 76
Permian-Triassic extinction event 68–71, 76
Pholidotamorpha 155
Pikaia 39, 42, 43, 52
placental mammals 154–5
plants
    arrival of 44–5
    flowering 74, 114–15

forests 56–7, 158–9
gymnosperms 92–3, 114
large 54–5
marine 44–5
mosses, lichen and fungi 48–9
pollinators 174–5
and soil formation 50–1
plesiosaurs 102–3
Pleistocene epoch 152
Pliocene epoch 152
pollinators 174–5
poppies 174–5
primates 166–7, 176–7
prokaryotes 10, 20–1, 22, 24, 26
Proterozoic Eon 10–29
pterosaurs 136–7
Purussaurus 164–5
Quaternary extinction event 188–9
Quaternary Period 152, 153, 188–9

rays 108–9
reconstructing 128–9
reptiles
    eggs of 62–3
    and mammals 101
    marine 82–3, 134–5
    in Mesozoic Era 134–5, 138–9
RNA 18–19

Saturn 12
sauropods 94–5
Schowalteria 140–1
sea snakes 135
seals 172–3
seeds 57
sexual reproduction 92
sharks 108–9, 156–7
Siberian Traps 68–9, 70, 90
Silurian Period 32–3
Smilodon 7
snakes 138–9, 162–3, 188
soil formation 50–1
Solar System 12–13
Spinosaurus 126
sponges 28
spores 57
Stegosaurus 98–9
Struthiomimus 127
Sun, The 12

taxonomy 24
termites 132–3
tetrapods 52
Therizinosaurus 127
theropods 96–7, 122, 123, 126–7, 19, 131
Tiktaalik 46, 60
Titanoboa cerrejonensis 162
tortoises 139
Triassic-Jurassic extinction event 90–1

Triassic Period 74, 78–9, 90–1, 94, 95, 139
Triceratops 124
trilobites 40–1, 69
tropical land vertebrates 84–5
tuatara 139
tunicates 43
turtles 139
Tyrannosaurus Rex 7, 98, 122–3

Uranus 12
Venus 12, 13
vertebrates
    arrival of 52–3
    emergence on land 60–1
    flying 74
    tropical land 84–5
viroids 19
viruses 19
viviparity 83

Walcott, Charles 38
walrus 172, 173
whales 6–7, 170
woolly mammoth 7, 178

Picture credits

Alamy: 46, 53, 69, 70, 75, 83, 84, 85, 86, 87, 89, 91, 99, 107, 108, 109, 110, 111, 112, 114, 115, 117, 118, 139, 139, 141, 143, 146, 147, 148, 149, 154, 155, 159, 162, 163, 167, 170, 175, 176, 177, 179, 181, 187, 189.

Axiom Maps: 180.

Fossil Wiki: 79

Lovell Johns: 159

Nix Illustration: 173

Public domain: 36, 49, 79, 105.

Shutterstock: 6, 7, 8, 12, 13, 14, 15, 16, 17, 18, 19, 20, 20, 23, 23, 24, 25, 26, 28, 29, 30, 33, 35, 37, 38, 40, 41, 42, 43, 44, 45, 47, 48, 49, 50, 51, 52, 54, 55, 56, 57, 58, 61, 61, 65, 66, 68, 71, 72, 74, 75, 77, 78, 79, 80, 82, 89, 90, 92, 93, 94, 96, 98, 100, 100, 102, 103, 104, 106, 107, 115, 116, 119, 120, 121, 122, 123, 124, 125, 126, 127, 129, 130, 131, 132, 133, 134, 135, 137, 138, 140, 143, 144, 150, 152, 153, 156, 157, 160, 161, 164, 165, 166, 166, 168, 169, 170, 171, 172, 173, 174, 175, 178, 179, 183, 184, 185, 186, 188,
Victor McLindon: 19, 27, 60, 67, 88, 101, 113, 136, 142.